Surviving the Revival

Ana Weaer

Surviving the Revival

A glimpse into the life of the
Weaver Family Band

By

Anna R. Weaver

ISBN: 1448608023
EAN-13: 9781448608027

Printed in the United States of America

Contents

Acknowledgements

This is probably one of the hardest pages to write in the entire book, but I'm going to try:

To my parents: Dad, I'll never forget your excitement and support the day that I flippantly mentioned I might write about our adventures in a book someday. Your input and suggestions were right on the mark, and my favorite part of the process was hearing you laugh at all the right parts. Mom, your prayers, support, and gentle encouragement gave me the inspiration and necessary nudge to finish it. Thanks to you both.

To my dear brothers and sisters: Y'all are my best friends in the world. You know all my quirks, yet you love me anyway. Thanks for giving me all this material to share, and for being such good sports about it. I love you guys.

To my uncle, Jim Weaver: Without your advice, guidance, and expertise, this book would still be a fantasy in my mind. I couldn't have done it without you. Thanks for taking this adventure with me.

To my grandma, Mildred Weaver: For her support, enthusiasm, and encouragement towards this project.

To the entire Senior Servants Sunday School class of East Orlando Baptist Church: For their support, encouragement, and inspiring desserts! (Love ya, Ms. Betty and Ms. Marti!)

To my grandpa, Art Parker: For his prayers and support towards this book project.

To my church family at Center Baptist Church: Your unending support, love, and encouragement mean so much to both me and my family. We truly thank the Lord upon every remembrance of you.

To my friends and spiritual family members at Mt. Yonah Baptist Church: We have a soft spot in our hearts for all the laughs we shared, fellowship we enjoyed, lessons we learned, and friends we made. Thanks for the memories and for being our very first fans.

To all the pastors, friends, family, and acquaintances who have contributed by way of stories, prayers, encouragement, and countless other ways. I can't name you all, but you know who you are. Thank you for all of your support.

And last, but definitely not least, to my Lord and Savior, Jesus Christ: Your love, grace, and mercy continue to amaze me. I'll never understand why You keep choosing to use me, but I wouldn't trade it for anything in the world.

This is your book, Lord, and we both know it. We did it!

PREFACE

A Personal Invitation

Well, hello there!

Welcome!

I'm so glad you decided to pick up a copy of this book!!!

Oh, you're still here? You didn't drop it like a hot tamale and run for cover yet? Great, you may actually have what it takes to get through. Let's just say that it's not for the faint of heart. Of course, neither is anything having to do with my family, but that notwithstanding, I'm just glad you've decided to stick around.

The opportunity to write this book fell in my lap unexpectedly, but it has certainly been an adventure. When I halfheartedly accepted the challenge, I knew it was going to be interesting, but I didn't realize how much I was going to learn about myself and my family, and how much I was going to grow in the process. Isn't it just like God to teach us life lessons by putting us in situations that only He could handle? Apparently, that's His preferred method of teaching me, but He still catches me by surprise when He actually brings me through it.

I'm sure you can already tell that this is definitely not going to be a dull, boring documentary. When I was laying out my plans, I knew from the beginning that I didn't want it to be journalistic, because that doesn't show you who we really are. If you've ever met my family, also known as "The Weaver Believer Survival Revival," or seen us in concert, you'd know that we're definitely not boring. Hyper-active maybe, but never boring. On the other hand, I didn't want this to be a plastic, everything-is-bells-and-roses "celebrity" biography either. We're a real live family. It's impossible for us be perfect, and we don't pretend to be. We just do the best we can. With us, what you see is what you get.

I want you to think of this as a personal invitation. Go ahead and imagine it: a thick, milky-white vellum parchment with raised gold lettering, the faintest hint of fragrant perfume wafting from the calligraphy-embellished, wax-sealed envelope. Never mind the fact that, in reality, it might be haphazardly scribbled on the back of an old, dog-eared church bulletin, with peanut butter and jelly stains on it for good measure.

Whatever shape it's in, this invitation invites you to take a peek behind the curtain--to catch a glimpse of us in real life. Let me put it another way. Some of our neighbors next door have three kids. One of them is a little boy... for sake of privacy, we'll call him Brian. When he was little, and Brian wanted to come to our house to play, his mom wanted to make sure that it was okay with us first. She told him to always check and make sure that he was invited before he came over. So, when Brian wanted to play, he'd stand in his yard and holler over: "Weebers! Am I 'bited?!?"

Dear reader, consider yourself officially 'bited.' I want you to feel like you've pulled up a Lazy Boy in our living room, a chair to our dinner table, or an extra seat in our van.

If you want a "behind-the-scenes" glimpse of our lives and our hearts, then just keep reading.

"Surviving The Revival" is different from other afore-mentioned biographies in another way, also. There's no ghostwriter regurgitating these facts for you. It's coming straight from the horse's mouth. Think hard, and you might be able to recall which Weaver I am. I'll give you a hint: I'm the acoustic bass player. Okay, fine--I'm the taller twin. Yeah, I thought that might help. I'm known as the quiet one of the bunch to most people, but you may be wishing that I actually *was* by the time this is over.

There is a saying: "Truth is stranger than fiction." Well, you're about to hear some of the strangest truth of your life. Strap in, because it's gonna be a wild ride!

CHAPTER ONE

Unbe-Weaver-ble

As cheesy as it may sound, we have actually been introduced to audiences as "Unbe-Weaver-ble," "the Von Trapps of Southern Gospel music," and the "Johnny Cash family" (because we all wore black). One time my dad was even introduced as "Big Daddy Weaver." That was definitely a new one. And it's not just on-stage, either. We've been likened to the Partridge family, the Duggars, the Brady Bunch, Eight Is Enough, and the Waltons. You name it, we've been called it.

There is a good reason for that, I suppose. For starters, we're a pretty big family. Mom, Dad, and eight kids tend to draw a lot of attention. And yes, people do stop and stare. Most of them do a head-count while they're at it. A walk through the grocery store can quickly turn into a parade. There's nothing like life in a fishbowl. Good, bad, or indifferent, there's nothing like it.

And if that weren't enough, we have something else that makes us stand out in a crowd. We're in a band. Not some of us, not most of us--every single one of us. The same band, too, amazingly enough. I guess that explains the musical references, huh?

We all sing, so we fall somewhere between a singing group and a choir. We all play instruments as well. We are a unique mixture of Bluegrass and Southern Gospel. We don't sing through our noses, but we don't sing to tracks, either. It's kind of a compromise. We play all the Bluegrass instruments: banjo, guitar, bass, mandolin, fiddle; but we sing more Southern Gospel than anything else.

Our name is pretty unique, too. It's "The Weaver Believer Survival Revival." What can I say? "The Singing Weavers" was taken. Actually, the name was born before any of us kids were. When my dad was young, he and his brothers would play their instruments together on the porch every weekend, and that name was one of my uncle's brainstorms. I'm willing to bet that this wasn't what he had in mind when he introduced it way back then.

Now, you may be asking, "Why on earth would you purposely name yourselves that?" Well, there's a story behind it, and my dad likes to tell it at every concert we perform. "We're all Weavers. We're all believers. Chris and I have eight children; we stand up here as a testament to survival. And, we hope to be a part of the revival that's going to sweep this country before our Lord comes back." How can you argue with that?

We started singing together almost 10 years ago, and we cut our first album 5 years ago. We've been singing semi-professionally and, later, professionally since then, growing in talent, experience, and showmanship every year. We now sing an average of 150-200 shows per year, and we sing all over the Southeast, with those boundaries stretching all the time. We've been to Alabama, Alaska, Arkansas, Georgia, Florida, North and South Carolina, Tennessee, and Pennsylvania. We try to sing wherever we're asked. We sing in churches, auditoriums, festivals, senior centers, gymnasiums, and music barns. You name it, we've probably sung in it. We sing in itty-bitty backwoods churches, and in churches that could moon-light as shopping malls. Wherever we sing, we do it for the glory of God. This isn't our show; it's our ministry.

So, that's who we are, and what we do in a nutshell. I'm trying to use this as an introduction; but, honestly, do you know how hard it is to introduce something like us? We're definitely not the norm. We rank up there next to "bizarre" and "pretty darn weird." You know what I mean? There will be chapters on how we started, what we're doing now, and everything in between later. But right now, I'd like to introduce everybody. Don't worry; there won't be a quiz on this, but it may help you get to know us better. That, or it may confuse you even more. Anyway, here we go:

Paul:
Rank: The Big Cheese, The Big Kahuna, The Supreme Chancellor. (You get the gist.)
Birthday: November 5th
Instrument of choice: Banjo
Vocal part: Tenor/Lead

Paul, better known as Dad, is our fearless leader. His sense of humor keeps everyone from getting too burdened down with the troubles of life. His love of music has been with him his whole life, and his songwriting skills show it. Before we started singing full-time, Paul made pewter chess sets and figurines, and he sold them at craft shows and such. He made all of the molds himself and casts, grinds, buffs, and finishes them in his own pewter foundry. Now that we're on the road so much, he can't make them as much as he used to, but some of his handiwork can still be seen on our merchandise table and at www.pewterchessset.com. In his spare time, his hobbies include reading, watching his extensive movie collection, and working on the next new song.

Chris:
Rank: The MOM (insert 'oohs' and 'aahs' here.)
Birthday: June 16th
Instrument of choice: Mandolin
Vocal part: Alto

Chris, better known as Mom, is the glue that holds us together. She books the concerts, keeps the calendar updated and current, and skillfully delegates the many chores and jobs necessary to run a family this size. She is also our navigator. She loves being a stay-at-home mom, even though we're not really home all that often! She's home-schooled us since preschool, so teaching keeps her busy, whether we're on the road or not. Her hobbies include keeping in touch with friends and acquaintances, networking on Facebook, reading, and swapping thoughts and ideas with other home-school moms.

Michelle:

Rank: #1
Birthday: August 17, 1988
Instrument of choice: Guitar
Vocal part: Lead

Michelle is our tomboy. She dresses up for the stage, but at home you'll find her in her favorite attire, jeans and cowboy boots. Her distinctive lead voice is irreplaceable in the band, as is her rhythm guitar-playing. Her role as sound technician keeps her busy on the stage, but when everything sounds great, she's to thank for it. Her hobbies include horses, motorcycles, cars, reading, drawing, and spending time with her dog, Sandy.

Anna:
Rank: Um, somewhere between #1½ and 2... (Seriously, do you know how hard it is to differentiate between twins?)
Birthday: August 17, 1988
Instrument of choice: Acoustic bass
Vocal part: Soprano/High Tenor

Anna is our creative mastermind. She's always coming up with new ideas, whether it's for new merchandise on the table, WBSR t-shirt slogans, story ideas, photo shoot angles, or whatever. Her bass is the heartbeat of the band, and her high vocals give the music a distinct sound and a sometimes ethereal quality. She runs the merchandise table and keeps everything stocked and looking good. Her hobbies include reading, writing, shopping, and trying to bring home every stray (animal, that is) that she comes across.

Sam:
Rank: #3
Birthday: May 2, 1990
Instrument of choice: any of them, but he prefers the banjo and fiddle
Vocal part: Bass

Sam is our musical genius. His expertise and enormous talents in the music area are invaluable to our band, even if they do give us license to professionally hate him every now and then. His songwriting abilities and deep, bass vocals give him even more of a distinction in the band, but we don't mind too much. His even temperament and comedian-like tendencies help to keep everyone calm. His hobbies include reading, learning new riffs and runs on any instrument he happens to have in his hands, and working out.

James:

Rank: #4
Birthday: January 20, 1992
Instrument of choice: Lead Guitar
Vocal part: Baritone

James is our rock star. His unique playing style and charisma onstage really drive audiences wild! He loves to be outdoors and can usually be found working on his yard, particularly the lawn. His assistance behind the merchandise table makes everything run very smoothly. He is also the one to go to if you need a good joke or funny story. His hobbies include working out, chatting with friends on Facebook, playing paintball with his brothers, and hunting.

Stephen:

Rank: #5
Birthday: June 11, 1994
Instrument of choice: Guitar
Vocal part: Alto

Stephen is our live wire. He is his own person and he's never met a stranger. His charismatic and energetic stage presence make him a favorite wherever we go, and he loves being on stage as much as they love to have him there. The songs he has written keep growing more and more popular as time goes on. His hobbies include hunting, fishing, and playing paintball.

Michael:

Rank: #6
Birthday: July 16, 1996
Instrument of choice: Stand-up Bass, i.e. Doghouse Bass, Bass Fiddle, etc.
Vocal Part: Melody

Michael is our quiet one. Well, most of the time, that is. His love to laugh and to entertain people usually overrides his quiet nature. His bass-playing and strong vocals make him an integral part of the band, and his help behind the merchandise table is very valuable. His hobbies include reading, fishing, exploring the creek behind our house, hanging out with his friends, and go-carting.

Sarah:

Rank: #7
Birthday: August 27, 1998 (Yes, she's 10 years and 10 days younger than Michelle and I. Just a little random trivia.)
Instrument of choice: Fiddle
Vocal part: Melody

Sarah is our artist. She's always drawing pictures or decorating her latest craft project. As one of the "little kids", the older folks can't help but be drawn to her, and she does a good job keeping Jonathan in line while onstage. Her strong, clear voice and winning smile makes her a favorite, too. Her hobbies include drawing, working on craft projects, and dancing to her favorite music.

Jonathan:

Rank: #8
Birthday: March 10, 2001
Instrument of choice: Guitar
Vocal part: Melody

Jonathan is our drama king. People have told us for years that he's going to grow up to be just like Stephen. Guess what? He is, but it's okay. Jonathan is our little entertainer. He loves to make people laugh. His practical jokes sometimes backfire when his brothers don't think they're very funny, but he usually charms his way out of trouble. His hobbies include playing outside, going to the kids' program at church, and swimming.

Well, there you go. You've met the family now. Are you thoroughly confused yet? No? Well, let's keep moving then. Things to do, people to see…

Surviving the Revival

CHAPTER TWO

Big Family Life

Some people would envision what we do as a form of edgy reality TV. Maybe so, but, for us, it is everyday life.

People, on occasion, don't really understand how we can live and co-exist the way we do. I can't tell you how many times people have come up to me and gushed, "Oh, I don't know how you can do that! If I had to be at home, or in the car with my sibling, parent, or child for hours on end, I'd kill myself!" Well, we've never known anything different, so I guess what we don't know doesn't hurt us.

Yep, living with a big family is quite an experience. It's definitely not boring. Dad has always said, "When you have one kid misbehave, you have an unruly child. When you have eight kids misbehave, you have a riot!" The man *does* have a point.

As a start, let me offer you a few of our statistics:

- Each month, 900 individual meals are served at our table, whether it's at home or on the road. (Calculate it up if you want: 30 days x 3 meals a day x 10 people = 900 meals. That's a lot of spaghetti!)

- 14+ loads of laundry are washed, dried, and folded every week. We have to put through at least two loads every day, or the laundry room becomes a wasteland. In the summertime, we have a clothesline that stretches from our back porch to a tree 60 feet away. It is usually full.

- Our monthly grocery bill runs between $450 and $600, depending on the sales going on that month.

- At any given time, there are at least five grades being taught in the same room by the same teacher, just like the old one-room schoolhouse.

- Our cooking pots closely resemble fifty-five gallon drums.

- The minimum price of going out to eat (and I'm talking McDonalds here; some of the kids are still satisfied with Happy Meals) is $65.00. Anywhere else is usually much higher.

- Unless we're properly rationed, we can go through a gallon of milk and two loaves of bread every day.

- When we're on the road, each of us kids gets exactly one-half of one of the bench seats in the van. "Home sweet home." On the bus, we get a bunk <u>and</u> a seat, but when you're bounced out of the top bunk at seventy-five miles per hour, you find out exactly what the smashed bug on the windshield feels like. It's safer to stick with the seats.

As you can imagine, big family life is a whole new kettle of fish for most people. They just can't wrap their heads around it. I'm sure there are times when it seems surreal. When our friends and relatives come to spend a few days with us, it's like a boot camp. Surprisingly enough, most of them *want* to come back, which I don't really understand at all. I mean, who in their right mind would want to wander right back into the jungle that they just escaped from? But, I digress...

Admittedly, a huge part of our ability to survive in a group like this is our sense of humor. If you can laugh at it, it can't be that bad--that's our philosophy.

Yet we have taken it to the next level. If you've ever been around our family, then you know how much we love to laugh. It's as much a part of us as our musical abilities. We take the verse in Proverbs, "Laughter is the best medicine," to heart. If that's literal, we should never have anything more serious than a slight sniffle.

The thing is, we'll laugh at anything. Nothing is sacred. Nothing is *untouchable*. One of our favorite things to do is to make each other laugh. It doesn't matter what we're doing: setting up for a show, sitting around talking, or even working hard. We still entertain each other. A quiet meal around our dinner table turns into a stand-up comedy stage on a regular basis.

We like to make other people laugh, too, but we know the limits of our own sense of humor. And we know exactly which buttons to push to send each other over the edge into complete hysteria. We must be the only family where one can playfully fling a biting insult, and receive a high-five, a chuckle, and a "Nice one!" for the effort. That, and an equally scathing retort, of course.

If it were a sport, I'd liken it to tennis, except that everyone has a volley of their own balls, a turbo-charged racket, and--there are no rules. The object of the game is to obliterate your opponents by sending them into fits of complete hysteria. Whew, if this were a contact sport, people might suffer. We'd also be in the Olympics.

As much as we like to entertain each other, we enjoy entertaining other people, too. If you've ever sat through one of our concerts, you know it's true.

Sometimes, laughter and joy can be a gift from God. When you're feeling down, He sends just the right person or thing to lift your spirits.

I suppose it can be argued that children in big families can suffer from an identity crisis. I disagree. I think that being in a big family pushes you to be a distinct, individual person with your own thoughts, opinions, and ideas, if for no other reason than to stand out from the crowd. How else can you explain, um, Stephen, and his multi-repetitive thoughts, opinions, and ideas?

I wouldn't trade my upbringing in this family for anything in the world. I believe that it has made me the best person I can be. I'm not the only one who feels this way, either. We all do.

Not surprisingly, there are some lessons that you learn when you're in a big group like this.

1. **You are a part of something bigger than yourself.** – Not only that, but you *represent* something bigger than yourself. In this case, it's your family. Picture this: you start cutting up, and you make a fool out of yourself in public. No big deal, right? It's only reflecting on you, right? Wrong! When you get home and nine other people form a lynch mob around you for making us, as a whole, look bad, you pick this idea up pretty quickly. This can also be applied

to being in a spiritual family. Is your behavior reflecting on it positively or negatively?

2. **Everyone has to do their part.** – In a family like this, it takes a lot of work to keep things running smoothly. As you read earlier, there's a lot of laundry and dishes. When one person doesn't pull their weight, everyone else has to pick up their slack or the whole group suffers for it. It's like a machine. When one cog doesn't do it's part, the entire machine is affected, sometimes to the point of injury or damage.

3. **When at all possible, get along with people.** – When you're stuck in the van for the eighth hour in a row, odds are you aren't up to being courteous to anybody. When you're spending the night in a tiny, smoke-scented hotel room that you're sharing with three other people, you probably aren't feeling very hospitable. However, everyone else is in the same situation, and lashing out at them isn't really going to make anybody feel better in the long run. By being tough and handling it the best way you can, you're doing everyone a service. One of Mom's favorite verses is "Seek peace and pursue it." – Psalms 34:14 (NIV). Take a guess how many times we've heard that one!

4. **You have to be flexible.** – In a group like this, it's very possible that plans are going to clash

from time to time. You can't get "bent out of shape" every time something doesn't go your way. It's not going to do anyone any good. Sometimes you just have to let things slide and be mature enough to keep your cool.

5. **To get noticed, sometimes you have to make a little noise.** – Let's face it, when you're one of the top four kids, you're okay when it comes to making decisions ranging from what music to use, to where we eat. But when you're number five, six, seven, or eight, you've got to squeak a little if you want anyone to notice you. I'm not just talking age here, either. It's also your level of importance in these decision-making roles. There was a time when I rarely offered my opinion of anything ... now they can't get me to shut up.

Apparently, I've figured it out. You can't expect people to value your opinions if you never share them. On the other hand, spouting off on everything that comes down the line isn't a great way to prove your advice valuable, either. You have to find some middle ground. You know, the neat thing about these lessons is that they work for everyday life, too. How many of them apply to you?

Surviving the Revival

CHAPTER THREE

Why We Do What We Do

A lot of prayer went into this chapter.

Not to say that I didn't pray over the other chapters, but let's face it: "fluff" pieces, funny stories, and anecdotes are a piece of cake. As a writer, you have complete control over where they're going to go, and what they're going to say. You don't have to worry that they will sound fake, or that you're just giving an easy, expected answer.

But life isn't always about anecdotes. Ours definitely isn't. Being in this big family, being in this great band, has its share of perks and fun times. But, as in everything, there are equal, and sometimes nearly overwhelming, drawbacks.

If we were totally honest about it, there are times when it would be easy to "call it quits." When you've just put your entire soul into your twelfth concert of the month, and you've barely made enough in total to pay the month's bills, it's easy to consider how much easier and steadier life would be if you held a regular nine to five job. And, don't you know, when you're at your weariest, most exhausted point, that's when the devil shows up, nonchalantly pointing out all of these things, darkly whispering how easy it would be to just give up. In those moments, one realizes exactly why s/he is doing this. Here are some of the questions we ask ourselves:

When you can barely scrape enough money together to pay the bills and buy just basic necessities, are you doing it for the money?

When you're driving around at one o'clock in the morning, trying to find a fast-food joint that's open, and you end up with a dried-out sandwich or a wilted salad from a grocery store deli that you take back to your cheap, smelly hotel room, are you doing it for the fun and exciting life?

When you're late running into a church on Sunday morning, slapping on make-up and yanking curlers out of your little sister's hair, while still trying to get everything set up before the service starts, are you doing it for the glamour?

When you end up singing to a crowd of twenty people who run for the door like there's a plague as you're playing your last song, are you doing it for the popularity or publicity?

I believe I can safely answer "No," if not "Heck, no!" to any of those situations, all of which have actually happened, by the way. That brings us back to the original question, ***Why?***

Why? Well, we sing because that's what God has called us to do. We know, without a shadow of a doubt, that this is what He wants for us. When He called us, we weren't performers; we were a young, but large family who could carry a tune and strum a guitar. We weren't anything special. We're much better now, but we haven't "arrived" at the pinnacle of talented glory anymore now than back then.

Fortunately for us, then and now, God isn't looking for talent. He is looking for "willingness." Sometimes all He's looking for is a heart, or a group of hearts, in our case, that's sold out to Him, no matter where He takes it. Look at Moses, look at Rahab, and look at Peter. All throughout the Bible, there are examples of ordinary people who let God take over. Because of that, He does incredible, extraordinary things through them. Hebrews 11 has been called the "Hall of Faith," and rightfully so. Dad likes to say, "God will either work through you or around you." His will is still going to be done, with or without you. But *you* will be the one who misses the blessing.

So, are we saying that we're saints? Heavens, no! There are times when we have fistfights over something as simple as the seating arrangements in the van! We're just ordinary people that God has seen fit to work through. It blows me away sometimes that God would condescend to our level and work through us, and, many times, in spite of us.

And a word to those who feel led to do this--anyone who's ever been involved in ministry, or is just seeking after God with their entire heart, it's no small can of worms that you have just opened. It's more like a Pandora's Box on steroids. The moment -- the very second you turn everything over to Him -- a Defcon 5 alarm goes off somewhere in Hell.

As a fully-committed seeker of His will, you are now a potentially hazardous adversary to Satan and his minions. You'd better prepare for attacks, because you now have a giant target painted on your back. And they're heading straight for your weakest points. I'm not trying to scare you off or create illusions. I'm just trying to give you a "heads up." The Bible says, Satan "is like a roaring lion, looking to and fro for who he can devour." Guess what? If he can get you so caught up with things that don't really matter (like self-doubt, or the opposite, self-obsession), he can keep you from doing what God has expressly called you to do.

It's really easy to get tired and battle-weary after constant attacks, but you can't give up. James 1:12

says, "God blesses those who patiently endure testing and temptation. Afterward they will receive a crown of life that God has promised to those who love Him." You can't give up now! We've already declared war. We just have to take our stand on the battlefield. You may have to take a few hits, but, overall, you will be victorious!

The Bible is chock-full of ways to ward off and withstand these attacks, and to win the victory over them. Ephesians 6:10-18 talks about the Armor of God. With His Word, His Armor, and the power of prayer, we can remain standing tall.

Please don't be discouraged, though. Oh, if I could only explain exactly how much you truly gain from seeking the Lord, and serving Him. There are blessings that you could never imagine, and power you won't even understand until we get to Heaven and God explains it to us. I must tell you--everything, even the worst, most painful sacrifice is worth it. Even while you're still here on Earth--it's worth it. Even on your worst days, it's worth it.

You haven't truly known peace until you're smack-dab in the middle of God's will. Even when everything is falling apart around you, and you're facing the fiercest opposition imaginable, you know, without a shadow of a doubt, that God's got it all under control. He's not sleeping or focusing on something else. He's there.

You're His child, and He loves you more than anything you could imagine. Psalms 37: 23 and 24 says "The Lord directs the steps of the godly. He delights in every detail of their lives. Though they stumble, they will never fall, for the Lord holds them by the hand." He's got you by the hand, and He won't let you fall.

If God is calling you, asking you to submit to Him, please don't turn Him away. You will regret it for the rest of your life if you do. It's the only way to know true freedom.

I know this chapter has strayed from the light, fun feel of this book, but sometimes things need to be said-- things that aren't always about "puppy dogs and rainbows." The truth is sometimes less-than-pretty, but it still remains the truth. I beg you to look deep. Are you doing what you've been called to do? Please don't guess. Be sure!

CHAPTER FOUR

In The Beginning

I'm sure you're wondering how this all began--how we got started as a band. Well, even if you're not, I'm going to tell you, so just sit tight.

Once upon a time, a long time ago…

Okay, I know that may be a little over the top, but sometimes it feels like a whole lifetime has passed since we got started.

We began singing together about ten years ago. We had some friends who would take us to sing Sunday School songs like "This little light of mine," "He's my rock, my sword, my shield," and other songs to shut-ins and neighbors. We kids had already been in a bunch of children's choir plays and productions, so we already knew how to sing in front of people, and we didn't sound half bad. We also went Christmas caroling as a family. Nothing like having a group like us show up on your holiday doorstep!

Dad, who already played the banjo and guitar, taught Mom to play the guitar, and we sang one song in front of our church when I was eleven or twelve. That was our very first public performance... and guess what? People liked it! We started singing more often, with Mom and Dad playing, and us kids singing as we stood in a line like stair steps. Well, we needed a band that was a little bit closer to the size of the vocalists, so we recruited two other guitar players, Marcus Milner and Larry Harbin, and a bass player, Jiffy Holland, from our church. We affectionately referred to them on-stage as "Uncle Marcus," "Uncle Larry," and "Cousin Jiffy." That worked well for about two years, until, in the same two-week period, all three of our secondary band members told us that they were moving.

Previously, we kids had been dabbling with various instruments, but we couldn't really play anything. Needless to say, instrument practice became a number one priority. That's when Dad really determined to turn us into a band. Because he didn't need eight guitar players, he collected a bunch of various stringed instruments, and we circulated around until we found what worked for us.

Let me tell you what we all started with:

Chris: Guitar
Anna: Guitar
Michelle: Fiddle
Sam: Bass Guitar

In The Beginning...

James: Mandolin
Stevie: Bass
Michael: Fiddle
Sarah: Auto-harp

Can you remember what we play now? Just in case you can't, I'll give you a list of our current instruments. As you can see, we played "Hot Potato" with them a few times and eventually ended up playing:

Chris: Mandolin
Anna: Bass Guitar
Michelle: Guitar
Sam: Banjo, Fiddle
James: Lead Guitar
Stevie: Guitar
Michael: Stand-Up Bass
Sarah: Fiddle

Granted, some of us received more instruction than others. Dad taught guitar and banjo. But for the fiddle, bass, and mandolin, we had to rely on outside lessons and/or learn-it-yourself books and tapes. Personally, I got four (count them--four) lessons on the bass before I was tossed into the group. Sink or swim!

The funny thing is this: several people told me when I was little, that one day we'd all be playing together. I can distinctly remember thinking, *"Yeah right, that's never gonna happen."* Surprise, surprise... it did!

Eventually, we got pretty good at playing and singing together. The novelty of our family was enough to get us into some local churches and senior centers. We sang a bunch of the old favorites and hymns, so many of the churches liked our style. As their interest in our family grew, we started performing more and more, going farther and farther to share our music.

At the advice of our pastor, Dad sat each of us kids down individually and had a talk with us. He asked us to prayerfully consider turning our hobby of singing and playing over to the Lord, to use however He saw fit. It might not go any farther than it was now, but God might decide to use us. It wouldn't always be easy or fun, he said, but he asked us to think and pray about it before we gave our answer. Personally, I remember going and doing just that. Eventually, and unbeknownst to each other, each one of us came back separately and gave him an affirmative answer. As a family, we turned our ministry over to the Lord. And that was it, we thought…

Well, that was like hitching your wagon to a rocket ship! When you ask God to use you, you'd better be ready, because He just might take you up on it. Interest in our ministry accelerated full-blast. A few performances here and there turned into 50 performances a year. As word spread of our ministry and our willingness to share, 50 shows turned into 100 a year. Obviously, we were getting too busy to do this part-time anymore, so we prayed about it, and again felt God's leading--this time telling us to quit our jobs and go into it full-time. It wasn't easy, but we did it. That was a few years ago. The next year, we had 150 shows. Last year, we performed 200 concerts. Apparently, God has more for us to do, because our musicianship and singing abilities have been growing as much as the interest in it. People constantly tell us "You're so much better than you were the last time you were here! We thought you were good then, but you were amazing this time around!" God's blessing is honestly what that is! We turned it over to Him and He's using us in spite of ourselves. Don't you love it when He does that?

We sure do, and we can't wait to see what's going to happen next!

Surviving the Revival

CHAPTER FIVE

Performing Live and In Color

In our line of work, we spend a large amount of time on stage, and we love it. One of the best things about performing is singing to a crowd who really enjoys what we're doing. There is no other feeling like it in the world.

And when I say "stage," I use the term loosely. The only thing that characterizes a stage is its location, not elevation. Sometimes they are the floors in the front or side of the room. Sometimes they're actual platforms. We've sung on stages that were two inches off the floor. We've sung on stages that were three feet off the floor. We've even sung on stages where there could be some real injury if one fell off. There's nothing like an "E ticket ride" from the stage down to the ground.

But, back to the point. We have been on all kinds of stages: church stages, music barn stages, and temporary stages for festivals and outdoor shows. You name it, we've probably sung on it. We've performed on tractor trailers, back porches, and even parade floats. I would like to share a few of our most memorable stages with you:

In Georgia, we were singing at a music barn where we had never performed before. We were on stage, doing our thing, when an older woman stepped out of the crowd and walked up to the stage, right in the middle of a song. We weren't sure what she was going to do, but there was little we could do about it. She walked all the way up to the front, stopped, and pulled a handful of money out of her pocket. This is still in the middle of a song, mind you. She threw it up on the stage, one dollar-bill at a time, then turned and went back to her seat. We were a little surprised, because this had never happened to us before. So we just kept on singing.

All of a sudden, several other people stood up and walked to the stage, followed by even more. Pretty soon, a crowd of people were walking back and forth to the stage, smiling and throwing money. Need I remind you, we are still in the middle of a song!!! How's that for distracting! As far as the little kids were concerned, this show was over! Jonathan, who was sitting in the crowd at that point, ran up on stage and started scooping up some of the money. Honestly, the stage looked like it had been made of dollar bills.

It turns out that this was what the crowd liked to do when there are kids in the group, especially when they really liked them. Well, we were sure surprised! We counted up afterwards and there must have been 200 one-dollar bills alone.

Another time, at the same music barn, we were scheduled to sing again. This time, we were ready for them. "Okay guys," we told the little kids, "let's not lose our minds like last time. If someone throws money at you, it's okay. Just keep singing and you can pick it up later. Let's be professional." All in all, it sounded like a good plan.

While we were singing, a small group of people came up and tossed some money on the stage -- not as many as last time, but hey, that's okay. Just keep singing. We were doing pretty well, when, from the corner of my eye, I saw something like paper floating down from the ceiling. It wasn't just me, either. Everyone, including the audience, was trying to see what it was. The people who ran the music barn had sneakily rigged a donation bucket to the joists of the ceiling. When they pulled on a string, the bucket emptied itself all over us. Again, another blanketing of money, but this one came from overhead. Michelle, who was in the center of the stage, got most of it on her head. Good thing it wasn't rolls of quarters! She'd have been a goner. Stevie, Michael, and Sarah were, again, hopelessly distracted. Jonathan just stood there with the most joyous expression on his face. You could almost hear the Hallelujah Chorus going through his head. He dropped to his knees into the pile and scooped it up, throwing it into the air as one would throw autumn leaves, much to the audience's amusement. Oh well, so much for the professionalism speech.

One time in Florida, we were onstage in front of a huge group of students. Unbeknownst to us, the stage guys had turned on a fog machine behind us. Imagine our surprise when we glanced back and saw smoke pouring from the soundboard! You have no idea how close we were to starting a mass exodus from the stage. Fortunately, we figured out where the smoke was coming from before we jumped ship, and ran out of the building, screaming "Fire! Fire!" You can take the hillbillies out of the country, but you can't take the country out of the hillbillies...

Speaking of professionalism, mishaps are another large part of the stage life. Let's just say that if it wasn't rehearsed, planned, or pre-prepared, it's usually a mishap. The key is not to let the audience know that it wasn't perfectly planned. For instance, we were singing a new song, trying to perform it without the music books. We did pretty well until we came to the second verse. We played the instrumental turn-around, stepped up to our mikes, and... nothing. Nobody could remember the lyrics. We looked at each other blankly for a century-long second, then Jimmy played the turn-around again and we sang the verse perfectly, looking to all the world like we'd planned the pause. Whew, that was a close one!

I can't tell you how many times we've broken strings on stage… especially Jimmy. He goes through so many; we call him the "String King." One time, we were singing at a big church for a televised service and on the first note of the first song, Jimmy broke a string. He didn't have any in his back pocket, which Dad had advised him to do beforehand. There was nothing to do but run all the way out to the van to get some, then run all the way back up on stage and change it there. Even Dad was running out of things to say. Jimmy now has a box of strings in his pocket every time he steps on stage. He can also change a string in less than a minute.

Here's another Jimmy story. Jimmy was in a hurry for a show one night. He grabbed his belt on the way out of the door and clasped it around his waist without running it through the belt loops, then forgot about it. Later, onstage of course, his belt slipped off and dropped to the floor with a clunk. Now, anyone else would be embarrassed, but what did Jimmy do? Stepped right over it and kept on playing. See what I mean? Professionalism!

Another time, Jonathan got a little too excited while he was singing and he slipped right off the end of the stage. Boom! It was like a cartoon. First he's there, now he's not. To the audience's enjoyment, he scrambled back up and kept on singing.

Then there was the time when the little kids dressed up for one of the songs, "Please Don't Send Me to Africa," in little leopard print costumes, complete with wooden spears. Well, one night, things got a little carried away. One spear bumped, then the other spear nudged, and pretty soon we had a war of the natives going on right in front of us on the stage. The wooden spears disappeared soon after that, replaced by inflatable ones. As you can see, life on stage can be interesting.

Probably the best way to show you our life on stage is to take you along for the ride. Figuratively, of course. We barely have room for ourselves in that van, thank you very much. Let's say we have a show at 7:00 PM on a Sunday night at a church that's about 2 ½ hours away. (This is assuming that we didn't have one that morning.) They want us to sing for about 2 hours. Now, most people think that it'd be pretty simple--get in the car, go sing, get back in the car, go home. But it's a little more complicated than that, I'm afraid.

You see, we have to plan backwards for a lot of stuff. Let me set out a timeline for you.

Saturday evening:

- Get all the show clothes out for tomorrow. Wash anything that needs it, and make sure they're all hung up and fresh.

- Call the contact person to make sure everything is still going as planned.

- Pack the instruments in their cases.

- Restock all CDs and merchandise.

- Gas up the van and hook up the trailer.

<u>Sunday</u>:

- 2:15 PM: Start getting ready for the show tonight. Wash up, get dressed, and make sure you're ready to leave at 3:00. Also, dress the small children and get them ready to go. Find something to keep yourself and others entertained during the trip. After you're dressed, go pack all of the instruments into the trailer.

- 3:00 PM: Head for the car. Run if necessary. Being late is not an option. Stragglers will be dragged to the car by their hair, if necessary.

- Around 4:00 PM: Stop for gas and bathroom break if necessary. (If not, you're just going to have to wait until we get there.)

- 5:15 PM: You've gotten to the church with a few minutes to spare. Meet up with the pastor, deacon, music director, caretaker, or whoever's in charge, then everybody helps to unpack the trailer using the assembly-line method.

- 5:30 PM: Everyone has their own set-up job: Michelle is in charge of the sound system. The others help with the general set up: setting up mike stands, getting out instruments, unreeling cables, and clearing the stage. My job is the merchandise table, usually set up in the foyer. Keeping everything stocked and set up, as well as looking nice, can be a challenge. Banners and other band-related decorations are set up in the foyer, as well.

- 6:00 PM: Time for a sound check. Everybody gets up on stage and adjusts their mike stands and instruments. We sing a song as Michelle adjusts the individual microphone and instrument levels.

- 6:15 PM: Finish any last-minute set ups.

- 6:25 PM: Have a prayer with the pastor. (We try to do this at every church.)

- 6:40 PM: Run to the bathroom for any last-minute makeup touch-ups, costume changes, etc.

- 6:50 PM: Take a seat in the front row. Use the moment to relax and prepare yourself for the performance.

- 7:00 PM: Pastor's welcome, introduction, etc.

- 7:10 PM: Showtime.

- 8:00 PM: Take a small break. The time is usually filled with a piano instrumental, a church member singing, or something like that. However, there have been times that we do the instrumental, take a deep breath, and keep on going.

- 8:55 PM: Sing closing song. Stand onstage as the pastor gives a benediction, his thanks, a closing prayer, etc. As the pastor prays, get ready to run to the foyer or front of the church so you can be at the table.

- 9:00 PM: Time to schmooze! Smile and talk to the audience, thanking them individually for coming out tonight and all that. Be as gracious, sweet, and charming as possible. Try to be available to whoever wants to talk to you, but try to spread your time around equally.

Also, if you're job is attending the merchandise table, you must do all of the above as well as assist purchasers with CD choices, give a commercial, if you will, about every piece of merchandise on the table, accept payment and give out the correct amount of change for their purchases, and everything that goes along with it.

- 9:45 or 10:00 PM: As the last of the audience trickles out, take a deep breath. Okay, break's over. Start breaking down. Whatever you did before, go reverse it now. You brought it all in and set it all up, now go break it down and carry it out. Put it all back in the trailer. Dad likes to quote Pa Darling from the Andy Griffith show: "All right, everyone, back on the truck!"

- 10:40 PM: Do a final sweep through the church to make sure that we haven't left anything or taken anything that isn't ours. Believe me, it can get confusing sometimes. As Dad likes to say, we steal only the very best.

- 10:45 PM: Head for home.

- 1:15 AM: Pile out of the car and into bed.

You see what I mean? It's not quite as simple as most people think. We've had people stay after concerts to help us break down and they're genuinely surprised. "You have to do this every time you sing?" they ask. "You sing all night, then you have to break it all down *before* you can go home?" Yep, as a matter of fact, we do.

While some of these times are estimations because every show is different, that's a pretty good idea of what we do on a given concert.

But you know what? We wouldn't trade it for the world.

Surviving the Revival

CHAPTER SIX

Illusions and Realities

I can't tell you all the times that people have come running up to us. "Oh, your life must be so glamorous!" they say, "It must be so wonderful! The traveling, the thrills, the excitement!" (Insert dramatic sigh here.)

Well, we always say the right words, but we're thinking, "Are you kidding?!?" Sometimes I can't believe the amount of people who actually believe this stuff!

I'm here to clear all that up right now. Yes, it can be exciting. Wonderful? Umm…uh…wait. Glamorous? Nope, not a chance!

That's why I decided to write this chapter. Its full title is "The *Illusions and Realities of being a Southern Gospel Superstar*," but I think that's a little too wordy for the table of contents. Not to mention, it's kind of imposing. Anyway, my purpose is to put a quick, painless death to some of the myths and rumors that have been floating around about celebrity life.

(No, I'm not saying that we're celebrities, but work with me, okay?) Here's a list of some common misconceptions, followed by some of the actual realities. You might want to take notes, 'cause this could get ugly. Here we go.

Myth #1: Superstars are Rich.

Illusion:

All superstars are unbelievably rich. Money just rolls in; so much that nobody even bothers to count it anymore. You have so much cash that, in your enormous mansion, complete with a pool in the backyard, and a nice little foreign car for every driver in the family, you have a room that is actually dedicated to your money. Green is the main color scheme. Banks come from far and wide to ask you to deposit some of that green into their companies. With this much money, you will never have to work again!

Reality:

I don't know if this dream world actually exists, but it surely isn't ours. Dolly Parton's maybe, but not ours. "Rich" is not synonymous with us at all. It would be one thing if all that mattered to us was money, but this is where the ministry part comes in. There are groups out there that charge several thousand dollars per night, and if it works for them, that's fine, but that's not our mode of operation. Not that it won't be one day, but we operate differently now. You see, a long time ago, we decided that we wouldn't charge for singing in churches. We would ask for a love offering and a place to sell our CDs. Other than that, nothing. We've always trusted God to take care of us. We have made exceptions, though -- for non-church functions, mostly. As sad as it is to hear, we have had a few take advantage of our willingness. On the other hand, God has done some pretty amazing things in places that we wouldn't consider to be good "payers." So, it all evens itself out. There have been times that we've left the house without enough gas money to get home if God didn't provide something for us at the concert. But, you know what? He has never let us down. So, are we rich? Well, I guess it depends on your perspective. We think we are!

Myth #2: Superstars get all the honor they deserve.

Illusion:
Silenced by the mind-numbing awe of being in the presence of superstars, your fans listen raptly as you regale them with stories of your Bluegrass-Southern Gospel band. Duly impressed, they simply cannot express how cool and amazing they think you are. They know they can only aspire to reach the level of prestige that you've attained.

Reality:
That scenario, on a much smaller scale, of course, only happens with an extremely limited group of people.

Think 1 in 500. With most folks, they seem mildly impressed when you mention that you're in a band, but when you say the word "bluegrass," their smile slowly fades. By the time you get to "Southern Gospel" and "family band," their eyes start to drift about, looking for an escape route to get away from these strange, "religious hillbillies." They can't help hearing "Dueling Banjos" in the back of their minds. And then there are the self-proclaimed "serious" musicians or vocalists who either laugh in your face, look down their noses at you, or icily ignore you; apparently offended by your very existence. Yep, that's prestigious for sure!

Myth #3: A Superstar's life is never boring!

Illusion:
Every day as a superstar holds something new and exciting! Fan club meetings, schmoozing with record label producers, interviews on radio and TV, attending parties as the guest of honor, not to mention sold-out concerts every other night! Even mediocre things such as shopping and traveling are turned into huge affairs, simply because you are a star.

Reality:
"New and exciting" turns into "day-after-day" very quickly. Singing, like any other job, is, in fact, a *job*. Arguably, the biggest part of the music business is done backstage anyway. The traveling, the setting up, the scheduling of concerts -- it quickly becomes routine. And let me just say this here, Bluegrass/

Southern Gospel isn't quite a "party-worthy" genre. It's probably more of a church homecoming genre than anything else. Not to mention, traveling as much as we do can be a real killer on your social life.

Myth #4: Superstars get to travel the world.

Illusion:
Using your "tricked-out" tour bus, you travel to your concert locations several hours in advance, allowing for plenty of time to sight-see and enjoy each town's flavor and flair. When you get to your concert's spot, you relax in front of your flat-screen TV in the air conditioning while your roadies get everything set up for you. Going cross-country? No worries. Just hop aboard your personal jet!

Reality:
Um, think 15-passenger van and a trailer. Think traveling at night. Think peanut butter and jelly sandwiches from the cooler. We put 40,000 miles on our van, and that was just last year! That's a lot of riding. And you'd better look fast, because the only sight-seeing you're gonna do is out of the van window at 60 miles an hour.

The only plane trip we ever took was to Alaska; a 10-hour "Red Eye" (all night, non-stop) flight. That was a load of fun. No, traveling isn't very glamorous or exciting after a while. All it turns out to be is long, long, long.

Myth #5: Superstars are the epitome of glamour.

Illusion:

After painstakingly selecting your wardrobe for the evening from a closet that could house a third-world country, you head off to an afternoon of prepping and relaxing in your in-house spa, complete with a giant bubble bath, facial, and manicure/pedicure, to get you in the mood to perform. Your personal hairdressers and make-up artists show up and transform you into the beautiful or handsome model that you're expected to be. They follow you around relentlessly until the second before you go onstage, powdering your nose so that you'll remain oil-free until you walk back offstage and into their capable hands.

Reality:

It's a good day when you can actually get your makeup finished *before* you get in the car. Those compact mirrors can be challenging; and you don't know pain until you've stabbed yourself in the eye with a mascara wand due to a wayward bump in the road. "Thanks a lot, Dad." And personal hairdressers? Please! We're lucky to get home to our hairdresser every six weeks or so before our haircuts grow out and we begin to resemble lumberjacks. And, you don't know panic until you're fighting for a place in line at the only sink in the house, with ten minutes before you need to be at the church. Yep, that's glamorous.

Myth #6: Superstars get all the groupies.

Illusion:

One of the best parts of being a superstar is the fans. The male band members are swamped by beautiful groupies, and the female band members' fans aren't too shabby either. Say hello to my friend, Tall, Dark, and Handsome! Because you're the superstar, they all want to be the one hanging off your arm. Your choices are unlimited, and there are always more where they came from if you don't really like your selection.

Reality:

I'm trying very hard not to laugh as I sit here writing this. There are many differences when it comes to secular and Christian music, but this is just ridiculous! Yeah, I'm sure that there are many very nice, interesting people of our own age who come to our concerts, but all too often, the nice, interesting ones don't come and talk to us. Mostly it's the ones who think they're a special gift to humanity that show up. (And let me insert a heart-felt plea here, "Good people, please come talk to us! We won't bite, we promise!") And we can forget getting to know any of the girls who happened to bring their boyfriends along. Good grief. Their eyes turn a lovely shade of green as they latch onto their beaus' arms, certain that Michelle and I will steal them away. That gets old after a while, too.

And don't get me started about the "stalkers." There's nothing like weird fans who are a little too... persistent. There are those who think you're just the greatest thing since sliced bread -- they're usually okay. The guys and gals that want to take you home with them, perhaps for a nice stay in their dark, dank basement -- they're a different story. Seriously, it's like a cross between Gomer Pyle and Hannibal Lector. Run! Run for your life!

Myth #7: Superstars have reached ultimate stardom.

Illusion:

Everyone fawns over you. Their sole existence is to cater to your every whim. You can do nothing wrong. Everything you do is excused, because, of course, you are a superstar. Fans pack into stadiums and conference halls, just to get a glimpse of you as you perform. Screams, whistles, and cheers erupt the moment you step on stage, and they don't die down, even after you run backstage. Afterwards, they flood the merchandise tables, buying anything that connects them to you, from a necklace like yours, to your latest CDs, to a lock of your hair on EBay. Fans run over each other as they beg for autographs, certain that life as they know it will end without one. You have reached ultimate stardom.

Reality:

Yeah, right. First of all, we play in churches... often! That's extremely limiting when it comes to crazed fans. Everybody is usually on their best behavior. Not too many "mosh pits" in the sanctuaries. True, we do get some grandmas trying to take us home, but that's about the extent of it. Secondly, "ultimate stardom" is a very versatile term. You're not excused from messing up. On the contrary, it's like living in a fishbowl. Everyone watches you with the vigilance of a hawk, just waiting for you to mess up. And no, locks of our hair haven't reached EBay yet. I've already checked.

Okay, are you getting the gist of it? Admittedly, these are based on some of our worst experiences, but there's still a grain of truth in each of these examples. I'm sorry if I burst a bubble about "showbiz" life, but you deserve a glimpse of our real lives, not just a fantasy of it. And if you're wondering why we do what we do, if not for any of this, you might want to skip back to the **"Why We Do What We Do"** chapter. You'll find the real reason there.

Surviving the Revival

CHAPTER SEVEN

Life on the Road

As you can imagine, a large portion of our time is spent traveling; whether or not we're working.

Long car trips were introduced at an early age. When we were little, the longest car trip we could imagine was the ten-hour drive from our home in North Georgia to Orlando, Florida to visit our grandparents a few times a year. If we only knew that it was an indication of things to come.

I'd say we spend an estimated average of two hours driving to every concert, sometimes more, sometimes less. Anyway, we spend much more time on the road than most people think.

On record, the longest trip we've taken is the Pennsylvania trip--a grueling fifteen-to-seventeen hour drive, which we travel over the length of one day. Why? Because Dad morphs into a "rest-stop Nazi" when it comes to long car trips, that's why! His philosophy is, "The sooner you get back in the car, the sooner you can get back out of it." Coming in at a close second and third are the trip to Arkansas, which is twelve hours, and the trip to Alaska, which was a ten-hour flight. No, we didn't drive to Alaska. Two weeks in the car is a bit more than I can handle. Just imagine it ... straightjackets falling from the overhead compartments. "Everyone please return your rubber seats to the upright and locked position."

Before you even ask, "No ... we don't take turns driving." Dad is kind of funny that way. He likes to be the one in the driver's seat.   He wants to "see it coming," in his words. A few years ago, someone suggested that he teach a few of us kids how to drive the bus. That way, "he could sit in the back and relax." "Oh yeah," Dad thought, "Put your eighteen-year-old daughters behind four tons of steel, and send them hurtling down the highway. Yep, that's relaxing!"

While we're on the road, the biggest problem is finding things to keep people occupied. When people get bored and tired of traveling, they get cranky or mischievous. There's not much in life worse than a six-year-old screaming, "He's touching me! He took my toy! He's looking at me funny!" as his brother laughs hysterically in the background. We try to avoid those situations at all costs. Unfortunately, chucking them out the window isn't usually an option. Neither is banishing them to the trailer, or the baggage compartments of the bus. Books, personal CD players, iPods, travel games, and travel DVD players are very effective and helpful. When all else fails, we play endless games of "Road Sign ABC", "I Spy", and "Find the State License Plate."

Not that we don't find other ways of entertaining ourselves. When they're bored, the boys have been known to wave wildly, complete with goofy faces, at any car passing by. It's an extra point if the person waves back, or drives off the road laughing. This can be very entertaining during a leap-frog traffic jam--you know, the ones where one lane moves, then the other lane moves, and so on and so forth.

One time, we were in one of the afore-mentioned traffic jams when a car full of cute college girls pulled forward in the lane next to us. Of course, the boys waved like palm trees in a hurricane. To their delight, the girls waved back. Now, if you think the boys were being goofy before, you can just imagine what they're doing now. Yep, being complete and total lunatics!

This went on for a while, back and forth, then the traffic began to break up, and we did the whole "stop and start" thing for a few miles. Imagine the boys' glee when the girls caught up with us again. This time, the one in the front seat was holding up a sheet of paper with a phone number written on it, which the boys instantly memorized as they sped past us.

After a brief tug-of-war with his brothers, Jimmy extracted the cell phone from the tangle of hands and worked up the courage to call. Finally, he dialed, everyone silently waiting in anticipation. "Hello," said a female voice. Jimmy opened his mouth to speak, but was cut off. "You've reached the Osteoporosis Hotline." her recorded voice said. "Please press 'one' if you'd like to talk to …"

Needless to say, Jimmy will never live that one down, though he is now known as our resident "ladies man." Ladies of all ages, that is.

Another facet of the traveling experience is the gourmet meals. Now remember, it costs us $65.00+ every time we stop to eat. Add that to the thirty-minute minimum of lost travel time, and you've got the reason we eat in the car… a lot! Peanut butter and jelly, bologna, and chicken salad are the main staples for sandwiches on any given trip, plus the best food group--junk food. Cookies, chips, pretzels, candy, Little Debbie snack cakes… oh, and apples and carrot sticks to be healthy, of course. At the beginning, everyone has a cup with his/her name on it, but towards the end, no one really cares, and they all get mixed up. I think I'm the only exception to that. Community cups? No thanks.

This moves us on to restroom stops. In addition to making two or three stops for gas during the trip, we also have to make a few stops for other reasons. Dad slips into that "Nazi" mode again here. "Fifteen-minute maximum, then back on the road. We only make a few stops during the whole trip, so you'd better take whatever chances you can get."

Rest areas are the usual stop of choice, mainly because of the size of the facilities, and the subsequent lack of lines. That helps us stay on our fifteen-minute deadlines. They're usually okay, but they sometimes have a war with gas stations over whose facilities are nastier. Just thinking about it sends a shudder down my spine. Ick!

There are times at these rest areas where we've actually run around the parking lot just to stretch our legs after being cooped in the van for hours. Races to and from the van aren't uncommon, either. It's better for the kids to be exhausted than to be bouncing around all over the car on a "sugar high."

Sleeping while we're on the road isn't an uncommon thing, either. Yes, there are times when we'll stop and stay in a hotel (more on that later), but when we're on a long trip, we try to get all the way there before stopping for the night, or early morning, as it may be. Actually, one of the best ways to travel is at night. The kids sleep, and the traffic is lighter. It's really not that bad when you think about it.

As you may have read earlier, each of us kids gets a half of a bench seat, totaling up to one and a half regular seats in the van during the day. But at night, that all goes out the window. The little kids, one placed strategically in each of the bench seats, are sent to the floor with a pillow and some blankets while the bigger kids get to stretch out on the seats. You gotta love the perks of seniority! There aren't many, but this is one of them. Oh, and don't feel too sorry for the little kids. They usually end up back on the bench seats before the night is through. Although you usually don't find out about that until your cramped arm or leg alerts you to the fact.

We usually don't drive all night, but we have on a few occasions. Even in those, we might stop for a few hours in the early morning, just so Dad can catch a quick nap before he falls asleep in the wrong place, and at the wrong time. He is usually okay with coffee and the little five-hour energy drinks, but we don't want to push the envelope there.

Nope, there's nothing like life on the open road. Sometimes it's a good thing, sometimes it's a bad thing, but regardless, it's a band thing.

CHAPTER EIGHT

On The Road ... Again

Another rarely-considered part of our travels is our spending the night in various places. When the options consist of sleeping at someone's house and getting a good night's sleep, or getting up at 3:30 AM to drive here or there, you can bet that staying over wins the vote by a landslide.

Hotels are a luxury, but let's face it, when you have to buy three rooms at a time each time you spend the night somewhere, it really cuts a chunk out of your earnings for the week. There is always the option of only getting two rooms, but since they really don't want you to put more than four people in one room, we'd have to start sneaking in like the Darlings on the Andy Griffith Show. Entering a few family members at a time helps a little, but it's still tricky.

Anyway, we usually end up staying at pastors' homes, various churchgoers' homes, in our bus parked outside someone's home or church, and occasionally, the church itself. Of course, it's always nice to have friends in the area upon whom we can descend like locusts, but that is not always an option. Or they pretend to be on vacation, as the case may be. Here are some of the adventures we've had:

Staying at a Pastor's/Churchgoer's House

One time, we were staying at a Georgia pastor's house on a Saturday night in order to sing at his church on Sunday morning. The house was small, but with this group, show me a house that isn't! He and his family were also musicians/singers, so we had a good time jamming with them until late in the evening. Afterwards, everyone went to bed, setting their alarms, and laying everything out so that it would be easily accessible in the morning.

We woke up at around 6:30 the next morning and noticed something odd. No alarms blaring, no nightlights blinking, no ceiling fans running. The only thing we heard was rain. Hmm. Upon further investigation, the pastor informed us that a storm had caused an apparent power outage. Now, that would have been bad enough, but this house was in a rural area. And in rural areas, when the power goes out, so does the water. Yep, there we were, desperately in need of a good cleaning-up, with a show in two hours. What to do? What to do? Well, we grabbed our cleanup kits and clothes, and piled into the van as the pastor called in reinforcements.

We arrived at the church, relieved beyond words that the power hadn't been knocked out there, too, and made a mad dash to look half-way decent. We actually didn't look too bad, considering that a few of us practically took a bath in the sink! The pastor's reinforcements had valiantly risen to the challenge, for, by the time we were ready, they had a nice breakfast buffet set out for us in the fellowship hall. No water? No problem!

Another time, we were in middle Georgia and the church set it up so that we could stay in one of the church member's homes for the night. Well, we assumed that it was going to be big enough to hold all of us. When we pulled into the driveway, though, we weren't expecting a MANSION! The preacher told us that he hadn't been to this house. He'd only been to her other house. Her other house?!? We walked in, and it was one of the most beautiful homes we'd ever seen. It looked like it could have come right out of *Country Homes and Gardens*. I swear, this house had so many beautiful antiques, it looked like a museum. The nice lady who owned it told us all about it as we settled in. Originally, the generous estate had been her grandfather's private 18-hole golf course. She was also a trophy hunter, so she showed us all of her monster bucks, elk, and caribou. Once we got things set up for the night, we were able to look around and explore. There was so much to see that it was almost overwhelming. We even found an original "Remington" painting hanging in one of the hallways. Actually, it was in the very hallway that the little kids were throwing a tennis ball for the lady's hyper Jack Russell terrier. Needless to say, we scrambled to put a stop to that. With this many kids, we knew something irreplaceable would get broken. Thankfully, nothing did. That was definitely an amazing experience, even if it was a little nerve-wracking.

Staying on the Bus

Staying on the bus is always an adventure. Just riding in it is fun. It's big, it's shiny... it's probably the closest thing we'll ever have to a limo! We all get to spread out and sit wherever we want. We can take naps or play a game. It's a nice change from the cramped van. You can also get pretty good at "surfing" it as you walk from the front to the back, or vice versa. However, if you're wearing socks, and Dad hits the brakes, you're going for a ride whether you want to or not!

The bus has 10 bunks, 18 seats, and a row of bench seats in the back, so you can sit or lay wherever you want. It also has a galley, a sink, a shower, and a commode. There's no such thing as rest stops when we take the bus. With a 125-gallon gas tank, we stop when we get where we're going... not before.

One of the drawbacks of staying on the bus is that it can get cramped pretty quickly. It's not too bad when you're riding, but when you get settled and everybody's stuff gets spread out, it gets small in a hurry. Probably the biggest disadvantage of staying and sleeping on the bus doesn't have anything to do with the space at all. The worst part is when Dad and the boys start snoring. In essence, the bus is like a giant tin can, so when the five of them start snoring, it sounds like bears in a cave … or Mack trucks idling outside your window … or a 747 trying to land on a tin roof. You get the idea. If you don't fall asleep before they do, your night is shot! Other than that, life on the bus isn't too bad, but I wouldn't want to live on it permanently!

Staying at a Hotel/Motel – (Not that we haven't had good experiences with hotels, but these are some of our worst.)

We were recording our latest album in Arkansas a year or so ago, and we opted to stay in a hotel for the few days instead of on the bus. The cost was the same once you added the price of fuel, food, and electricity. Not to mention, it's much nicer and much less cramped in a hotel … or so we thought.

Anyway, Jon Raney, the person recording our music, took care of all the details. So when we exhaustedly arrived at the studio, he took us over. When we got there, the rest of us waited in the car as Dad, Jimmy, and Mr. Jon went in to get the room keys. We sat there for a while, then we began to notice something odd. The people who kept coming out of the hotel lobby seemed to stumble to their cars, almost as if they were … drunk. Most of them couldn't get into their cars on the first try. Uh-oh!

Meanwhile, in the hotel foyer, the boys began to notice the friendly but inebriated patrons and the sign that said "See Bartender for rooms." Oops!

Our recording technician was mortified, but we'd already paid for the rooms, so we had no choice. We learned later that he hadn't been there for a few years. It used to be a hotel with a nice restaurant in it. Not anymore! His wife told us later that she couldn't believe he'd done that. "You took them … to a bar?!?" she'd said. Well, with no other choices, we decided to check out the rooms before we made any decisions. One was out front, and the other was in the back. The one in the front wasn't too bad, besides being down the sidewalk from the bar. The one in the back was a different story. It was the biggest, but you had to go down a long, scary staircase and a dark alley to get there. That one also had a bullet hole in one of the windows, patched neatly with silicone glue. Scary!

Fortunately, we were only there at night, and it was only for 4 days, so we didn't have to stay for too long. It's a good thing, too, because on that first night, the police showed up, apparently questioning people up on the second floor. On the second night, the air conditioning went out, and the shrieking ceiling fan murdered all our hopes of getting a good night's sleep. The next night, a bunch of bikers showed up, and it sounded like a Harley Davidson convention was going on outside until 3:00 AM. It was a good thing that we left the next day. We were afraid to see what was going to happen next. We will always have the memories of staying in a hotel with a bar.

Another time, we were spending the night in a hotel in South Georgia, graciously paid for by the church we were singing in the next morning. Our cousin, Jessica, was along for the trip. You know how it's easy to find things to amuse yourself when you're bored in the car? Well, we were pointing out the dumpiest looking buildings that we passed. We passed one hotel that looked pretty run-down, shabby-chic at best. As we passed it, Jimmy joked, "I bet that's the one we're staying in." We all laughed. All of a sudden, we stopped and circled around. Yep, that was the one we were staying in. The joke's on you, Jimmy.

Anyway, it wasn't really that bad, other than the fluorescent yellow painted walls of one room and the other room's neon orange walls. We chose rooms, laid out clothes, and went to bed. The next morning, we girls woke up and found a HUGE cockroach lying upside down underneath the air conditioner vent! (Bear in mind that there was another vent just like it right over my bed!) Ewww! Michelle, our brave and fearless defender, was in the shower, so we made Sarah put a plastic cup over it. We passed through the rest of the morning preparations in denial of the roach's existence until Michelle finally came out and disposed of it. Boy, do we know how to have a good time.

Staying at a Church

I just want to say, "There's something spooky about churches at night." In the daytime, they're the most beautiful, wonderful, bright buildings ... but at night, they get scary. It's one thing if it's full of people. It's a whole different thing entirely when you're alone. Maybe it's the oppressive silence. Maybe it's the cool, clammy temperature. Maybe it's the shadows of dead choir members on the walls (an ode to Mark Lowry here) ... I don't know, but it's something.

Anyway, there have been times where we've had to stay overnight at the churches where we were supposed to sing the next day. That's always interesting. It's kind of hard to fall asleep when you're looking out the window at a tombstone, or when a picture of Jesus is staring down on you. I'm not going to lie, it gets creepy. We usually make it through though, and staying busy helps. Most of the time in those situations, we set up all the sound system and stuff, so we won't have to do it in the morning.

One time, Michelle and Sam were setting mike stands up in the dark sanctuary ... alone. They were doing pretty well until they heard a loud "whoosh!" from the ceiling. Now, if it'd been me, I'd have high-tailed it out of there before whatever it was decided to make friends, but they stood their ground, even if they did jump out of their skins. We still don't know what it was. We think maybe it was the Holy Ghost.

We usually take over a few Sunday School rooms to sleep in, so we're not spread all over the place. Air mattresses and more recently, cots are used a lot. I'm glad we've moved up to cots, because there's nothing like waking up on a flat air mattress on the hard floor to make you want to serve Jesus the next morning. (Don't look so spiritual... you know what I'm talking about.) Those are the days that you have to pray for a little extra grace and time for a nap later. And coffee ... lots of coffee. Have you ever noticed that the older you get, the more uncomfortable an air mattress or cot gets? Maybe it's just me, but the more I sleep on them, the more I love my bed.

When we do stay over at night, we have to be careful, because people show up at the most inopportune times. We've had people come by late at night (like that won't scare you to death!) and early in the mornings, not to mention everywhere in between. You have to keep things from being spread all over the place, too. Wherever you are, you'd better make sure that you're decent, though. It's kind of hard to explain exactly why you were running around half-dressed at church, especially to the little old lady who comes in early to prepare the Sunday school lessons. Those are just the occupational hazards.

Our life on the road, both day and night, can be a real adventure.

CHAPTER NINE

Meeting the Rich and Famous

Throughout our travels, we've met many other people who do what we do. The Gibbs family, The Bruce Weeks family, The Stevenson family, Due South (a great bluegrass band)--the list goes on. Sometimes, though, we actually get to meet someone "rich and famous." (Insert 'ooh' and 'aah' here.) Keep in mind that I am using the term "rich and famous" loosely. Let's just say that anyone who's richer and more famous than us falls into that category. There are times when that could count for the majority of the country.

Anyway, let me give you a few examples off of our list:

Dr. Sam Cathey (well-known evangelist)

The day for which we had been preparing for weeks had finally arrived.

A few months before, we had been offered the opportunity to perform at a casual luncheon for the legendary evangelistic speaker, Dr. Sam Cathey. While that honor, in and of itself, made us nervous, we had an extra worry, too. Our brother, Sam, had written a song called, "If You Don't Want the Devil to Get Your Goat, Don't Tell Him Where It's Tied," coining one of Dr. Cathey's signature phrases. Would he like it? What would happen if he did? What would happen if he didn't?

With those questions in mind, we agonized over the songs we thought would be best, what we should say, and so on. By the time we got to the lake house where the First Baptist Church of Alamo, Georgia was serving the luncheon, for which Dr. Cathey would be speaking later that evening, we were nervous wrecks. After our customary prayer for God's blessing, we brought in the instruments for a warm-up before Dr. Cathey arrived.

We were sitting around and picking a little when we received a special request: "Old MacDonald had a Farm" by an adorable 2-year old boy named Brett (name changed for privacy.) Unable to resist his big brown eyes and shy smile, we gave it a try and came up with a pretty good rendition, if I do say so myself. So there we were, singing about the cows mooing and the ducks quacking, with Brett singing and clapping along with gusto, when who should walk in but Dr. Sam Cathey himself! Well, we were too far into it to quit now, so we sang until we ran out of verses, with Dr. Cathey watching us the entire time. "More, More!" he cried as we finished, grinning and clapping ... so we did just that. We sang until lunch was ready, and while we ate, Dad filled him in on the story of our band. After lunch, we played Sam's song for him, which he loved, and played a few more of our original songs for him. Every time Jimmy would go off on a guitar run, Dr. Cathey would watch him in amazement, then shoot him a huge thumbs-up when he was finished. We weren't scheduled to sing before he spoke at the revival service that evening, but his outburst of "Well, why in the cat's hair not?!?" got us a speedy invitation. So, we sang that night and had a blast doing it. While I don't necessarily recommend singing nursery rhymes for someone that you're trying to impress, why not? It worked for us!

Karen Peck and New River

Another time, the Southern Gospel group, Karen Peck and New River, was performing at a church in the area. We hadn't seen them in person before, so we decided to go.

Now, I'm a firm believer that bad things happen when you sit in the front pew. You Baptists know what I'm talking about. There's nowhere safer than that back row. There have been injuries, and even casualties amidst the mad and crazy race to get there every Sunday. Seriously, it's like an invisible target is painted on your forehead when you move into that up-front location. There's just something about it.

Anyway, back to the point. We were at the concert and trying to find a seat. Guess what was available? You got it--the front pew. Mom and Dad and the little kids were cowards, and beat a hasty retreat to the second row, leaving us older ones smack-dab in the front. It was a great concert. We clapped and sang along with everybody else. Then came the ending song. You know, the one where people in the audience get called up to sing with them? Yep, you know where this is going. Michelle got called up, and sang the ending chorus and a couple of reprises of "Robe and Crown" into Susan Peck Jackson's (Karen's sister's) microphone.

God, in His grace, knew that I couldn't handle a situation like this, so Michelle got to be the lucky recipient. Well, maybe that, and the fact that I was ducking under the pew during the selection process. *Don't make eye contact! Don't make eye contact!*

Now, am I saying that the things that happened were bad? Well, no, but do they ever happen to the people sitting in the back row? I think not.

Gerald Wolfe (of the singing group, Greater Vision)

We had a concert one night in Morristown, Tennessee. There was a pretty good crowd coming in and we were excited about it, until a friend let us know that he'd invited Gerald Wolfe, the lead singer of the Southern Gospel group, Greater Vision, to attend. Of course, we immediately panicked but skillfully disguised it behind our show faces. Yeah, right.

When we got up to sing, there he was, slipping into the back pew a moment or two before we started. (See, there it is again! Back pews = safety, no matter who you are.)

We can't help but look back on this meeting with a little bit of chagrin. No, it had nothing whatsoever to do with Gerald Wolfe. It had everything to do with the fact that, when this event occurred, we were terrible! We did the best we could that night, but it was, in fact, quite a few years ago. We weren't even close to the caliber we are today. When we met with him later, he was incredibly gracious and supportive. Who knows, maybe we'll get to meet him again one day. Maybe we won't embarrass ourselves this time.

Truett Cathy (owner and founder of the Chick Fil A restaurant franchise)

One time, we got invited to play for The Annual Bluegrass Festival at the Rock Ranch in Barnesville, Georgia, which is owned by Truett Cathy, the owner and founder of the Chick Fil A restaurant franchise. We didn't really expect to see him. His age had made it difficult for him to travel as much as he used to. Anyway, we *did* get to meet him. He drove up to the stage in a little white golf cart, his wife along for the ride. We even have the pictures to prove it! He must have given us fifty "free chicken sandwich" coupons. They came in quite handy one time when we were in Maryland. Times were kind of tough, and we weren't sure that we could handle another peanut butter sandwich from the cooler. We finally convinced Mom to go into a Chick Fil A, armed with ten coupons and big, dark sunglasses. Surely they wouldn't mind giving away ten sandwiches during the lunch-hour rush, would they? Actually, I wouldn't know. I was hiding in the van with the rest of the group.

Frank Cox (pastor of North Metro First Baptist Church, former president of the Georgia Baptist Convention, and former 1st Vice President of the Southern Baptist Convention)

I'm not quite sure how, but somehow our church convinced Frank Cox to come and speak to our wonderful, but rather small, congregation (compared to his church) in Robertstown, Georgia. It was during a revival, and we were asked to play the special music before the preaching for one of the evenings. We ended up playing one of our new songs, "We Are All Part of the Body" for him later in the evening. I guess he liked it, because he preached a sermon that had a lot in common with that same topic the very next night. We had a good time visiting and getting to know him that week.

Other "celebrities" that we've met and performed with are The Dove Brothers Quartet, Triumphant Quartet, and the Mike Lefevre Quartet. They were very gracious and supportive, even when they didn't really need to be, and we learned many things from them.

Well, there you have it. That's about as far as we can go for this chapter. We've run out of 'rich and famous' people to talk about. Who knows? I may have more to write about next time.

Surviving the Revival

CHAPTER TEN

We Just Love Old People

I'm sure you've heard the song, but, you know, there's a ring of truth in that phrase. Even before we started singing professionally, we have always had a deep appreciation and love for older folks. They have so much wisdom to share. I mean, they've lived their lives. They've made mistakes and learned lessons. Sometimes we forget that they were our age at one point, too. As far as I'm concerned, people need to stop traveling to find monks in the mountains of Tibet to find wisdom, and just look to their parents and grandparents for it. You'd be surprised at the timeless knowledge that they possess. Yes, I know that there are exceptions to the rule. I've met my share of them, but there are so many wonderful grandparent figures out there, and I've met my share of them, too.

One of the reasons that we like seniors so much is because we grew up under so much of their influence. We have good relationships with our grandparents, but

Chris's family lives in Alaska, about 5,000 miles away, and Paul's family lives in Florida, about 500 miles away. So, because of the distance, the majority of the day-to-day "grandparent" influence we had while growing up came in a form of surrogate grandparents that we had at our home church. We had great relationships (and still do) with many great people at both of our home churches.

The other great influence that we had while growing up came in the form of a few neighbors who lived across the field from the house where we lived. It all started almost accidentally. When we were young, a group of seniors: two brothers, Ross and Guy Palmer, their sister, Lucille, and Guy's wife, Polly, would walk around "the block", as we called it. It was a dirt road that trailed around the field and pond, eventually circling back to our house. They would pass by our house almost every morning. We eventually began taking a break in our school days about the time that they came by, and we walked with them almost every morning. We never ran out of things to talk about. But, our favorite times were when Ross, Guy, and Lucille would regale us with stories of their youth, of making mischief, surviving during the Depression, and growing up in such a different era than our own. We loved spending time with them, and were heartbroken if we ever missed a day. We learned so much from them, and we didn't even know it at the time. We had to stop our walks when we moved away from there several years ago, but we still love to see them whenever we can, and we will never forget the memories that we made with them.

Usually, our family is really popular with seniors and senior groups, mostly because of the novelty of cute little children, and because our music has an old-fashioned, traditional sound to it. That and the fact that we don't have drums. The devil's in the beat, you know. I can't tell you how many times I've heard that observation over the years. To be honest, the difference between the bass and the drums is "what" exactly??? Anyway, because of those reasons, whatever they are, we're often invited to perform for many church-based senior adult groups.

They're usually fun, and the people are usually very kind and gracious. It's always interesting during luncheons when we all end up seated at different tables. I guess they're surprised that teenagers and kids can hold intelligent conversations. It's very tempting to say, "Well, stranger things *have* happened!" but we usually can hold it together. Let's just say that the people sitting at Stevie's table will never forget it. Think of it as a scarred-for-life thing.

There was this one time that we were scheduled to sing for a senior adult group in Tennessee. They had around 250-300 members, so we were singing in their church's huge sanctuary. We got there early, with plenty of time to set up, and we spent an hour and a half setting up and perfecting our sound system. When it was time to sing, we powered up the system ... but a country song came blaring over the speakers. Apparently, this church's system sometimes picks up the frequency from the radio station across the road, and when we ran ours through it, the amount of power on the stage amplified it. Of course, by the time we figured it out, it was too late to fix it. Dad tried to start with the introductions anyway, but it's hard to take yourself seriously when your monitor is blasting a female country artist singing, "I'm here for the party!" Well, we ended up just turning it off, and singing as loud as we could to project to the audience. We all still laugh about the time we went to the seniors' group "for the party."

Nursing homes, assisted living homes, independent living homes, and senior apartment complexes are also a large part of our seniors outreach. They usually aren't "paying" gigs, but we do them to keep in touch with the ministry part of our band. We usually perform at 1-2 of these establishments a month, sometimes more than that. Dad started the tradition, and now we all agree. "Even if we weren't musical, they'd sit there and listen to us beat on pots and pans just to be able to see the children," he says. There's no blessing like bringing a smile and a bit of happiness to someone's life. They are so gracious, too. We just love being able to bring back good memories for them.

We've had quite a few "home" adventures, too. There's an assisted living center in Georgia that we've been to about 4 or 5 times. It's quickly become one of our favorites. I'll never forget the first time we went there. We got there and set up, expecting the usual sweet-but-subdued crowd. Boy, were we wrong! We started an up-tempo song, and all of a sudden, a couple of the seniors jumped up and started dancing! Soft-shoe dancing! Can you imagine how distracting that was? Well, needless to say, we kind of stumbled through the song. The looks on the little kids' faces were priceless! You could see the questions in their eyes: "Gasp! What do we do now?" especially when they were invited to dance, too. That was the closest thing to a mosh pit we've ever had. Well, more people join in every time we go there, even the home directors one time! The kids have gotten pretty good, too. We've learned to just go with it. Now, everyone looks forward to going to the "dancing nursing home."

Another time, we were singing in a nursing home in Pennsylvania. Mom kept thinking that she recognized one of the residents, but she couldn't figure out why. After the concert, she started talking to him and found out that he was one of her old college professors when she attended The King's College! Boy, was she surprised! They had a good talk, and he thought that what she was doing with our family was great. Later, she told us that he looked the same way that he had when she was sitting in his Economics class that unspecified number of years ago. (Hey, I've got to keep her happy here!)

Yet another time, we were at a nursing home in Florida, singing for the residents. The directors had informed Mom earlier that they would be serving refreshments to them during the show. Well, we assumed that they would be serving finger foods and maybe soda or juice or something like that. Well, they served juice all right, but it was a little more fermented than we'd been expecting. Yep, there were carts full of beer and wine rolling through the room! Talk about a senior's keg party! I bet that took the ache out of their bones. It was a lot of fun playing for them, too, 'cause every time we did a song that they liked, they raised their Dixie cups and yelled "Cheers!" and toasted us. They laughed at all of our jokes, too. Boy, that one was fun!

One of the most infamous of our nursing home visits has been the one where we met Nelson. We were in Lancaster, Pennsylvania, after a concert, when Nelson walked up. At 6' 3", with broad shoulders and weighing in at about 200 lbs., Nelson wasn't quite the "little old man" that one would expect to find at a nursing home. He came clunking over with his walker and a comb-over that was more of a comb"up" than "over." Think of a long, white spike job. "Let's see some of those CDs," he demanded. I showed him what we'd brought, reading off the songs of each of them in great detail. "I need to go get some money," he said, "How long will you be here?" Michelle told him that we'd be here for a little while longer, but Nelson apparently heard: "We'll be here for approximately 1.5

minutes and then we're leaving and we're never coming back, so you'd better hurry, hurry, hurry, Nelson!!!"

So, Nelson headed for the door to the hallway, but was held up when he had to wait behind one of the slower-moving residents; a little old man, as it were. "Sometime today!" he growled at the offending man. But when the little senior failed to move faster, Nelson had had enough. He slammed his walker to the floor and screamed "Get out of the way, darn it!!!" One of the attendants quickly ushered the man out of the doorway while we watched on in utter disbelief. Nelson took off like a shot, making incredible time for an old man with a walker, screaming obscenities to anyone unfortunate enough to get in his way. He returned in the same fashion, but this time bearing two $5 bills. I was hoping to give him the CD he wanted, and beat a hasty retreat, but it was not to be done.

He couldn't decide which CD he wanted, so he was off again, after politely instructing me not to leave. Yeah, like I was gonna move *anywhere*. I don't think I would have moved if the building was on fire and burning down around me.

The wait was longer this time, but I was frozen to that square in the carpet. "Take all the time you want, Nelson." I kept thinking, "No rush--just please don't scream at me!"

Several attendants stopped by during my wait; just to let me know that Nelson would be coming, and that he would like to buy some CDs, so please don't leave.

Yep, that's what their mouths were saying, but their eyes were screaming: "Please don't leave before Nelson can get a CD! Our lives won't be worth living if you do! Please, oh, please, oh please, oh, please!!!" Even they were afraid of him! "Yes," one of them smiled sympathetically, "He's one of our less patient residents."

Finally, I heard him coming, both from his grumbling and growling down the hall, and from the horde of attendants coming to run defense. This time, he had an older woman in tow, who fished the money from her purse. Where he got her, I didn't know, nor did I care. All I knew was that if he started screaming at me, I was gonna cut my losses, throw the CDs as a diversion, and cut a trail out of the nearest door. I cannot begin to explain to you the relief I felt as Nelson, grinning like a kid with candy, finally bought his CDs, bid me farewell, and started back down the hall.

I debated about putting this one in here, but I was out-voted. Another infamous story comes to mind when I think about nursing home escapades. One time, we were in an assisted living home in Florida, and we were meeting and greeting the residents after the show. An elderly woman came up and started chatting with Mom. "I'm 97 years old," she said, smiling. At Mom's perfunctory "ooh and aah," the woman leaned in conspiratorially. She said, "You know what keeps me so young?" Mom replied that she didn't know. The lady declared, "No shopping and no sex."

Before that day, I'd never seen my mother absolutely speechless, but, that day, she was. The best part was that the woman thought she was whispering it, but her voice carried much farther than she'd planned. By the end of her declaration, Jimmy's face had turned purple as he tried not to burst out laughing. The chicken wing Sam had been eating was now located in his left lung. Michelle stared off into space, refusing to make eye contact with anyone. I was suddenly overcome with a fascination for the lovely tile work on the floor. Fortunately, we held it together until we got back to the car. Then we proceeded to laugh until we cried as the little kids asked "What? What?" over and over. Well, what were we supposed to say after that?

Ah, things are never boring in the senior circles. Some of them are like kids--you never know what they're gonna do or say. All you can do is smile and nod.

Surviving the Revival

CHAPTER ELEVEN

Name That Lyric!

Since the beginning of our band's existence, we've always sung songs that we'd heard other bands sing-- finding the ones that we liked, and tweaking them until they fit our style. In the past three years or so, we've begun writing some of our own music. It started out with Dad as the main songwriter, but as we kids have gotten older, and God has blessed our talents, Sam and I have also begun to write original songs, with Stevie quickly following in our footsteps.

"Now, where do you come up with these songs?" you may ask. "How do you come up with such diverse and unique topics?" (I mean, let's face it--"Don't Let the Devil Get Your Goat!" is not your typical song title, and that's just one of many examples!) Well, in answer to your questions, we don't choose the topics, themes, or genres of our songs. There are some lyricists or songwriters who can say, "I'm going to write a country song about love today," and go do it. We're not those kinds of writers. Most writers *aren't,* for that matter.

It's one thing if you're just going to write a fun, little, fluffy song. All you need is a cute set of rhymes. But in order to write a song that has the potential to bless and/or challenge its listeners, God has to inspire it. We just have to take them as they come. As Dad likes to say, "God writes the song; I just push the pencil." And it's true. That's just the way it works for us.

Songs can show up in the darndest places, too. Dad wrote one song between sales at a craft show once. Sam had one pop up right in the middle of an unbelievably busy concert tour through Pennsylvania. We had 19 concerts in 13 days up there and, still, something new managed to sneak in. One time, I had the lyrics of a song come to me right in the middle of a concert. I had brand-new lyrics running through my head *while* I was performing! Needless to say, I was a little bit distracted. Hopefully, I didn't make too many noticeable mistakes.

You can't always decide what you're going to write about, either. I mean, you can have your own ideas about what you want your song to be about, but ultimately, God is the one who inspires it. That's the main reason why we have so many unique, thought-provoking songs.

When we first started writing, each of us songwriters worked individually, writing all of the verses and choruses, and composing the music ourselves, before we brought the new song to the band. Recently, however, we've developed what we call a "caucus," or core group of writers. Now, whenever one of us has a song with some potential, such as a completed first verse and chorus, s/he can bring it to the caucus of writers, which is composed of Paul, Chris, Sam, Anna, Michelle, and Stevie. Together, we combine our various talents and efforts to produce a finished song. Do you have any idea how much easier it is to write a song with the assistance of several other creative minds? It is immensely easier, let me tell you.

Everyone in the caucus has an individual talent or strength to contribute to the group, besides, of course, coming up with good, inspiring lyrics that also happen to rhyme, which is a feat in and of itself. For one of our more recent songs, we wanted to touch on the phrase "genie in a bottle." Do you know how hard it is to find a rhyme for "genie?!?" When all we could come up with was "meanie," "beanie," and "weenie," we took a caucus vote, and decided to go in a different direction.

Anyway, back to the subject at hand: personal strengths. Here they are:

Dad's strength is the conviction and message behind the songs' lyrics. There have been times when we've called him "Brother Weaver" when he started getting preachy, but he usually isn't very amused.

Michelle helps us find and keep the tempo and melody of the song without getting lost. She keeps us on track.

Mom painstakingly records or writes down every little word or chord change to be sure that we don't forget any of it.

Sam's vast musical talents help to develop the melody and tune of the song.

Let me add a note here. Everyone has equal parts in developing lyrics. That should go without saying, but I will mention it anyway. Okay, are you happy, guys?!? Now, back away from the laptop.

My strong points are my English skills. I am a wordsmith, so I am good at coming up with synonyms--new or different ways to say the same thing in hopes of finding a good rhyme. In short, I'm the dictionary and thesaurus. It's good to have a skill, I guess. (That definition was for those of you who ... let's just say you have that "glorious lack of sophistication" as Jeff Foxworthy so eloquently puts it. Hope it helped!)

Another division of the caucus can be separated into two groups: the radicals and the pacifists. An easy way to show you the difference between a radical and a pacifist is to gauge his or her reaction to one of our more controversial, for lack of a better term, songs, *"We Are All Part of the Body."* "How has it achieved this pinnacle of greatness--this distinction?" you may

90

ask. I'll just write down the whole chorus and you'll get the idea.

"We are all part of the body,
We all have a job to attend.
We are all part of the body,
Try not to be the rear end, my friend
Try not to be the rear end."

Got the gist of it?

Now, when a radical hears this song, he is thrilled, immediately thinking of all the people that need to hear and apply it. The pacifist, however, is shocked, thinking: "Gasp! Oh, Heavens! They just said 'Rear End' in church! Can they do that? I hope no one is offended! Let's sing 'Jesus Loves Me' instead! Everybody likes that one!" They both know that there's truth in the statement, but they have vastly different ways of saying these things. The radical will spit it right out, while the pacifist will probably use more subtle tactics to get their point across. Not that pacifists won't take action on it. They'll just have to psych themselves up in order to do it.

As hard as it is to believe, pacifists are a grossly-outnumbered minority in my house. Actually, anyone who knows us, at all, has no trouble believing that. In case you couldn't tell, I'm one of the select few. Most of the time, anyway. Add Mom in, and that's our entire outnumbered group.

Amazingly enough, we have found that pacifists play a very important role in songwriting. Strong messages in songs are very important if you want to be taken seriously. But if the message is too harsh, or "in-your-face," your listening audience will shrink pretty quickly. For example, the radical has a song with a great message, but it's a tad rough on the edges. Enter the pacifist. He wants the message to go across as much as the radical does, but the pacifist will try to soften and smooth out those edges as much as possible. It's a lot easier to accept an idea when it's handed to you on satin instead of sandpaper. It's funny how that also works with life, isn't it?

All in all, only a radical could write something like "We Are All Part of the Body", and only a pacifist could write something like "Jesus Loves Me." It's when the two mix that amazing things happen.

CHAPTER TWELVE

Two Pigs, a Goat, and a Joke

Here's a rhetorical question: Has anyone, whether it be a parent, grandparent, friend, relative, etc., ever announced your lack of a romantic relationship to more than, say, a dozen people at a time? If the answer is no, you should immediately be on your knees, thanking God for His kindness and benevolence. If this scenario has actually happened to you, (1) I'm so sorry for you, but (2) take all the feelings of embarrassment, awkwardness, and utter mortification and multiply it by ten, then you will have caught up with my twin sister and me. My father has announced our status of singleness on every stage, in every week, in every month for about eight years. Amazingly, we haven't really had any lasting side effects, except maybe when "good old dad" spouts the fact that we've never been on a date in front of a bunch of young people. Then my smile glazes over, my right eye starts to twitch, and I hear a roaring sound in the back of my skull ... Well, maybe not that bad ... but close!

And actually, "no," I've never been on a "real" date. Michelle hasn't, either. It's not because we're extreme introverts, legalistic, or too unattractive to merit a second glance. A walk through the grocery store--THE GROCERY STORE--is enough to disprove *that* theory. God just hasn't brought the right young men along yet. Michelle and I were raised with high standards, and we don't want to waste our hearts, memories, and lives on substitutes for the right person. We're not stuck up. Nor do we think we are better than anyone else, but those are just our personal convictions. Michelle likes to say: **"We have a strict no-losers policy."** It can't get any more plain than that.

Anyway, enough of that "rabbit trail" and back to the story. One of Dad's favorite jokes to tell on stage is how he wants to get at least "two pigs and a goat" for each of us when we get married. Can you imagine being traded for two pigs and a goat? *There's* a real ego boost for you! While he is only kidding, it's still a pretty strange and absurd concept to consider. I don't know where he came up with that, but he's been saying it since we were little. I guess it seems logical to him to share it with the rest of the world, too.

I will also add Dad's favorite part of this joke too, even though, since you are reading this book, you've probably heard it at least once. Anyway, here it is:

Dad: "Well, we were at the Smith family reunion in Athens, Georgia. For those of you who don't know, the

94

Smith family has almost 600 members. We were out in the middle of the field on a flatbed trailer, because we were the entertainment for the day, when I told the joke about two pigs and a goat. Now, there was a young man sitting on a fence and there were goats out in the field behind him. He went "Yahoo!" and he jumped off the fence and started running for the goats. (Audience laughs here.) When we finished and went backstage, Michelle came up to me and said, "Hey Dad?"

I said, "What is it, Honey?"

She said, "I just wanted you to know that if that "Gomer" shows up here with a goat on a rope and a handful of flowers ... you're a DEAD man!"

(Audience goes into complete hysteria here.)

There you have it--the most laughed-over joke in the whole set.

As you may have noticed, Michelle is a little more open about her feelings and opinions than I am. Dad calls me a closet rebel ... let's just say that Michelle requires no closet.

Anyway, in almost every concert, there is either a parent or grandparent or, occasionally, a young man himself who decides that it would be funny to "offer a trade" for one of us, all in good fun, of course. We've been offered a Mustang convertible, a few church buses, Indian ponies, cows, rifles (the boys had a difficult time turning that one down), goats and pigs, of course, and countless other things. We've had women coming up and showing us pictures of their sons and grandsons, describing their wonderful qualities and attributes. We've also acquired a sizable collection of assorted stuffed farm animals, mostly pigs and sheep. Apparently, stuffed goats are hard to come by. Now some people may be offended by all this, but we just laugh and go along with it. It keeps things interesting, so we don't mind.

One time, we were in Pennsylvania, performing at an outdoor concert. We were in Pennsylvania Dutch country, so every now and then, an Amish buggy would go by, and they would stop to listen before heading on their way. The most interesting part occurred when a buggy full of young Amish men passed by. Michelle and I were sitting on the front row, getting ready to go up on stage when we heard, "Hi, girls! Hello! Hi!" We looked over and all the Amish guys were hanging out of their buggy, waving at us as they went by. We didn't know what to think! I don't know about you, but that didn't fit my idea of Amish young people at all!

The only major drawback to this joke occurs sometimes when we're in backwoods, country churches. You know, out in the Boonies. You know it's time to leave when Dad tells the joke and nobody laughs. You can almost hear them ciphering … "Two pigs and a goat, huh? I think we can prob'ly swing that price right there!" That's when you paste on a smile, threaten your brothers with certain death if they leave your side, and do the best you can. No joke! In one of the afore-mentioned mountain churches, I had the visiting revival preacher, who must have been over 100, tell me, "Girl, if I was 18 or 19, every time your mama threw the dishwater out the back door, it'd hit me square in the face!" How do you respond to something like that?!? A stifled chuckle and a sweet smile, that's how!

I'm telling you, you can't make this kind of stuff up! Life with this group can be crazy, but at least it's not boring!

And honestly, sometimes I wonder when God is going to bring the right guy into my life. Believe me, waiting is hard sometimes. I have little old ladies come up to me all the time saying, "Honey, have you tried E-Harmony?" or "Don't feel bad that you don't have a boyfriend, dear, God will bring the right one in His timing." I've even had people tell me that I should lower my standards. Well, thanks for the advice, but no thanks. I know that a lot of people don't understand this at all, but I've turned it over to the Lord.

That may seem stupid to some of you, but I know that since God's in control of everything else in my life, I can trust that He'll take care of this area, too.

Surviving the Revival

CHAPTER THIRTEEN

Angels On My Shoulder

"All night, all day,
Angels watching over me, my Lord ...
All night, all day,
Angels watching over me."

Yes, it's just an old camp song, but you might be surprised at how God has kept a protective eye on us throughout the years. I'm basing this chapter on the myriad of ways that God has taken care of us, whether it was financially, physically, emotionally, or spiritually. He always comes through with exactly what we need (not necessarily what we want) when we need it. We can always trust that He'll do it according to His timing.

I can't begin to count all the times that God has taken care of us, carried us through some trial or danger or crisis. And that's just the times that I personally have seen Him at work. I'm sure there are some that we won't know about until we go to Heaven and finally see the big picture. However, I want to share with you some examples of His protection and provision:

Physically:

Do you want to hear some amazing numbers about our family? Try these on for size:

Number of broken bones: 1

Number of sets of stitches: 3

Number of hospital stays: 7 (but since these were for childbirth, I don't think they should count.)

No, that's not this year. That's through *all* our years. It sounds unbelievable, but this is one of the ways God takes care of us. We're just like everybody else. We get sick, too, and the "big family rule" of sharing is definitely not in our favor. But, for the vast majority of the time, we miraculously have a few weeks without any shows on the calendar to recover. Not that we haven't performed while we've been sick; we have on several occasions. God always gives us the strength to get through it, though.

On the Road:

I can't even begin to estimate all of the times that we've been late, or gotten lost, or been held up for some reason, only to pass a vehicle accident exactly

where we would have been, if we had been "on time."
We've had accidents happen right beside us, behind us,
or in front of us, that we miraculously escaped. We
spend so much of our time on the road, especially in
bad weather, poor driving conditions, and congested
traffic, we could very easily be involved in an accident
or injury at any time. But God always takes care of us.

One time, we were taking one of our first trips with the
bus, and we took a wrong turn. Well, we were late, and
we couldn't find a big enough place to turn around on
this little mountain road, so Dad pulled the bus long-
ways across the road to do a three-point turn. No
sooner had he blocked both lanes, when two tractor-
trailer trucks came speeding down the road. Both of
them slammed on their brakes, tires squealing as they
came at us in both lanes. I thought we were gonna die
right then and there. Amazingly, Dad got us out of the
way before they slammed into us. But you can't
convince me that there weren't a few angels heave-
ho'ing us out of the way.

And don't think that we don't have car trouble every
now and then, either. With so many hours spent on the
road, we're bound to have a few problems. One time,
we were on our way home from a concert at a church
when one of our rear tires blew. We got off to the side
of the road, and the boys tried to figure out how they
were going to change it without messing up their show
clothes. Not two minutes later, the pastor of the

church, who was four cars behind us, pulled over with us and helped us change the tire.

Another time, we were on the way to another church concert and our radiator blew up. So there we were, stuck and stranded, with no way of getting us to the church, much less our equipment and instruments … and we were still 50 miles away.

Well, we got on the phone to the church and, no sooner had we apprised them of the situation, than people started showing up to get us and our stuff to the church, back home, and to help us figure out what to do with the van.

See what I mean? He takes care of us.

Spiritually/Emotionally:

By reading this book, I'm sure you've already heard some of the downsides to being in a ministry. Getting burned-out is one of the biggest ones. When you don't want to go any farther, when you feel tired, frustrated, or ready to quit, the idea of turning your back on the whole thing can be very seductive and enticing. *"Just think,"* that little voice whispers, *"think how easy it would be just to tell God to find someone else for the job… that you're too tired or frustrated to do it anymore. It is your life, after all."* That temptation can get very strong indeed. But, it's in those moments that God brings in exactly what you need to keep on going. Believe me, we've experienced them.

One time, we were getting ready for our fourth show of the weekend. It was a rainy, dreary Sunday night, and we were exhausted. You know, after one of those nights when it seems that your alarm goes off two minutes after you close your eyes. The last thing we wanted to do was to climb into that van again. For a wooden nickel, we all would have voted to stay home. However, we had made the commitment, so we had to go.

In the van, Dad said, "You remember when we first asked you guys if this is what you wanted to do? When we said that there would be days that you didn't want to do it anymore? Well, this is one of those days, but we're gonna have to make it through the best we can." We said a special prayer along with our usual one, asking God to give us extra grace and strength to get through the concert.

I will never forget that night. We trudged in there, set up, and when we started playing, the crowd almost tore the roof off the building. They whooped and hollered and clapped and sang along the entire time. After almost every song, they were on their feet, yelling and clapping. They liked each song better than the one before. Let me tell you, we were walking ten feet off the ground when we left that night.

In the same way, when we're at our most exhausted point, that's when God sends the little old lady, the refreshed pastor, the in-tune-with-the-Spirit churchgoer who says just the right thing, gives just the right words of thanks, and prays just the right prayer of blessing over us.

That's just the way God is. When you think you can't take it any more, He's there to refresh and empower you even more than you can imagine, and it's usually at your darkest moment.

Financially:

I don't even know where to begin here. There have been so many times that God has taken care of us financially that I'm at a loss for where to start.

God has taken care of us financially from the beginning. When Michelle and I were born, we were seven weeks premature, so we had to stay in the hospital for three weeks, racking up a $70,000 hospital bill. Because of that, our whole family grew up without much money. Even way back then, He was teaching us to rely on Him.

One of the ways He takes care of us financially is through gifts and donations. There have been many days when the "wolves were at the door," and we had nothing to pay them with. However, there was a check in the mailbox that covered the exact amount.

Love offerings are the same way. We have had times when we've gone to shows, not sure if we'll have enough gas to make it home. He always provides. It's not just in the big churches either. We've been in large churches that barely give us enough to make it home. At the same time, we've gone to tiny, little churches and been given a surprisingly large amount of money compared to the number of people present, and it all goes to the glory of God. He always provides what we need, and He loves to do it in impossible, unexpected, and unexplainable ways.

Odds are that some of you have done some of the things mentioned above. So if you are one of the many people who have contributed to us, and our ministry, we can't begin to thank you enough. God has worked miracles through you. Thank you for being willing to be used by Him.

Prayer:

Prayer is also a huge part of our protection. We've learned never to underestimate the power of one praying person, or a group of praying people. We pray together as a family, and with the pastor if possible, before every concert we perform. We believe in the power of prayer so much that we ask people to pray for us everywhere we go. When this book is finished, I'm going to try to get a weekly or monthly newsletter up and running. Do you know what will be a huge part of it? That's right: prayer requests. James 5:16b says,

"The earnest prayer of a righteous person has great power and produces wonderful results." Prayer is one of the most powerful weapons God has given us. We need to use it to the best of our abilities, instead of turning to prayer when nothing else works.

And so ...

Let's face it--being sold out to the Lord is a *dangerous* decision. The devil would gladly destroy our family to stop us from spreading God's love and encouragement, if God would permit it. I'm sure it would be easy to let that fact alone stop us from fulfilling our potential as Christians. However, being in the center of God's will is the safest place we're ever going to be. Obviously, God has something planned for us, because He keeps protecting us and providing for us like nothing you can imagine. Personally, there's nowhere I'd rather be.

So if you're also in this position, you can be sure of God's provision, even if you're under persecution. If nothing else, being under Satan's attack should convince you that you're heading in the right direction. You're apparently shaking somebody's plans up.

One of the great things about God is that when you surrender to His will, He will always take care of you. He'll move mountains, put food on your table, and give you angels as bodyguards. He'll give you rest beneath the shelter of His wings and the strength and power to stand strong in His name, even under the strongest attacks. He'll bring you through. Just trust Him for it.

CHAPTER FOURTEEN

Just For The "Record"

We can look back now, with our six released CDs, to when our former pastor and trusted friend, Chris Pearce, suggested that we make our first CD. We can't help but laugh at our terror and ignorance. You see, back then, way back in 2004, we couldn't even fathom such a project. We weren't singing full-time yet. We'd only been singing and playing together for a few years. Our idea of "recording" had been standing in front of Mom's ancient gray tape player/recorder to make practice tapes of new songs that we were trying to learn... not exactly the most high-tech equipment!

Dad almost laughed it off, but the idea planted itself in his head. It just kept growing, becoming more and more appealing. Now, it just so happened that we had an acquaintance, Mr. Lamar Canup, whose hobby was recording, and who, subsequently, had his own studio in the basement of his house. (Don't you just love how God orchestrates that kind of stuff?) When Dad approached him about taking on our project, he was very gracious and happy to help us out with this new and exciting undertaking.

You should have seen us the first night that we went to his studio. We were as nervous as "a long-tailed cat in a room full of rocking chairs." (Hey, I'm from the South ~ Country clichés come with the package.)

Mr. Canup was so gracious and patient with us as we struggled to understand what exactly we were doing. ("Wait, you mean we actually have to sing *into the microphone*?!?") After he explained the possibility of using isolation booths, in which everyone had to sing and/or play separately, he watched our eyes glaze over at the mere thought, so he decided to do things a little differently. We lined up and stretched out across the main recording room with a minimum of one mike in front of each of us, and we recorded. You almost couldn't tell that we were nervous, except maybe the loud whoosh of released breath after the "all clear" call at the end of the song.

At the time, we thought our first album was the best thing we'd ever heard, but now we can hardly stand to listen to it without cringing. This has nothing to do with Mr. Canup's talent and abilities, of course. It was our sorry excuse for singing and playing! We just weren't very good … that's all there is to it. Perhaps we are our own worst critics, but I guess that's better than being an overzealous fan; "Pride goes before the fall," and all that.

Well, our first CD was such a hit at concerts that we decided to make another one shortly after--a "Christmas" one this time. For personal reasons, Mr. Canup was unable to record with us again, so we were back to square one. God provided another studio. This one was under the direction of John Grimm, another great recording technician. It was situated behind his quaint music store in Dahlonega, Georgia. We recorded our second and third albums, "Sunday Singin' 'Round the Tree" and "Sunday Singin' On the Road" with him.

Because of the smaller spaces of this particular studio, we learned a new way of recording: laying down individual vocal tracks. While we still played the instrument tracks together, we split up to record the vocal tracks; each of us singing individually. That opened up a whole new problem area to deal with ... boredom. Seriously, many an evening went like this:

Get up, sing your part for one song, and go over any areas that need work. Then, you sit and wait for everyone else to lay down that song before you can move to the next song, which could take hours (and has, at times!) Now, the innovative part is finding something to do with all that time. We were forty-five minutes from home, so it's not like we could go back and chill until it was our turn again. So, we had to find creative ways to entertain ourselves quietly when we weren't recording.   Personal DVD players, books, games, cards ... you name it, we've used it.

Perhaps a little rundown, a "dictionary" if you will, of recording terms might help you understand what we had to learn:

- When you're recording a CD, it's called either an album or a CD project.

- The term used when referring to individual recordings is "tracks."

- The person who records your tracks is called the recording technician.

- "Laying down a track" means recording it, whether it's recorded on a tape or digitally.

- "The 'All Clear' call" is what the recording technician tells you when he has stopped recording your track.

- Vocal recordings are called "Vocal Tracks" and instrumental recordings are called "Instrument Tracks".

- "Mixing" is the term for putting the vocal tracks and instrument tracks together and balancing them together for production.

- CD projects that have been fully mixed and completed are called "Master recordings" or just "Masters".

There you go. Do you feel so much more knowledgeable now? It was a real learning experience for us, let me tell you!

We actually met up with Jon Raney, our current recording technician, while we were recording with John Grimm.

We were looking for someone to print our "promo" pictures for us, and his company came up in the list. When we told him what we did, he immediately requested that we contact him the next time we wanted to record, so he could bid for the job. So, in 2007, we did. With his price quote, we determined that we could record two CDs at the same time for a cheaper price than one at a time. So, we packed up, and headed to Arkansas. It took us a week to record both CDs, and we headed home with two finished masters. We've been with him ever since, and now have three great new CDs to show for it.

Raney Recording Studio, a family-owned, third-generation recording studio, is located in Drasco, Arkansas. By a literary show of hands, how many of you have been to, or at least know where Drasco, Arkansas is? *No one?* I figured as much. There's a reason for that, too. Jon told us that they had originally been based in Nashville, but that they routinely had problems with recording artists disappearing for weeks at a time. The singers would just find something or someone to spend that time with, or get "lost" in Nashville's night life. So Raney Studios made an executive decision to move to their hometown, Drasco. There, an artist *had* to focus on music, simply because there was nothing else to do. This is not a joke! There is a gas station/bank/convenience store/pizzeria, all encompassed in one small building for your convenience, along with a movie rental place, a diner, and another gas station. That's it! There's nothing else to distract you from your music. Technically, Drasco isn't even a town. It's a township--a collection of counties and mini-counties. But I must admit … that diner food and pizza from the gas station was amazing.

In the Raney Recording Studio, recording sessions start around 9:00 or 10:00 AM and usually go until late in the evening. It takes us three or four days to record a ten-song album--one day for laying down the instrument tracks, one day for laying down vocal tracks, and an average of two days for mixing. We split up for all of the tracks now, and we use huge headphones in the several isolation booths.

The recording console in Raney studios is roughly the size of a Mack truck. It takes up almost half of the rather large studio room. Seriously, it could be confused with the command deck of the Starship Enterprise. There are all kinds of bells and whistles that hum and/or make unusual electronic sounds, plus lights and buttons that flash, blink, and flicker at their leisure. They even have sliders and switches that move by themselves during the recording process. And you're supposed to pay attention and stay focused during all of this!

We've also learned a few tricks of the trade. When we recorded our latest album, "Sunday Singin' On the Mountain Top," almost all of us were fighting a vocally debilitating cold. "Was it really that bad?" you may ask. Well, let's face it, when singing is your career, any form of cold or cough can be vocally debilitating. Anyway, we've discovered ways to hold such infirmities off. We drank enough hot coffee to keep us up all night just to clear our throats. Hot cranberry juice, while definitely an acquired taste, will strip your throat of anything vocally debilitating. A spoonful of honey will soothe a stripped throat, and allow you to keep singing. In a pinch, cough drops dually strip and moisten your throat. These are just the kind of things you learn when you're in the business. I'm sure there are other vocal fix-its too, but these are the ones we know and use the most often.

I have a fun piece of trivia for you now. When we recorded our Christmas album, "Sunday Singin' 'Round the Tree," we totally botched one of the songs. After we finished slaughtering it, we all laughed and elbowed each other about how bad it was. Unbeknownst to us, the recording technician kept the tape rolling, recording our whole tirade. When we heard it, it was too funny, so it actually ended up on the album! I won't tell you the song, but if you listen for it, you can probably find it!

So, is recording as easy as you thought? Probably not, but I'm willing to bet that it's not as hard as we imagined it would be, either. Nice compromise!

CHAPTER FIFTEEN

Walking on the Wild Side

Our family is full of pet lovers. And we've had all of them over the years--cats, dogs, birds, fish ... never any rodents or reptiles, but that is Mom's decision, not ours. She's funny that way. Anyway, because we live in a rural area, animals of all kinds aren't really foreign to us, but I thought you might enjoy hearing about the adventures with nature that we've had on the road.

Holy Ghost Wasps

One time, we were at a church in South Georgia, singing for their Homecoming. Traffic was terrible that morning, and we were a little late, but for once it was okay, since we weren't singing until later in the afternoon. Anyway, that's how we ended up in the balcony. It's amazing what you can observe from up there, if you look hard enough.

There we were, listening to the sermon, when we began to notice something a little strange. There was an unusually large number of black wasps in the sanctuary. Now, we've been to a lot of older churches, and it isn't uncommon for a few wasps to find their way inside, especially during the summer. Well, this wasn't a *few*. This was a few dozen! There must have been 20 or 25 wasps hovering over the crowd. Every now and then, one of them would attempt to make a landing on some unsuspecting church-goer, followed by a hushed, but frantic explosion as the poor person tried to dislodge his unwelcome pew-mate. Even in the balcony, we weren't safe. One of the wasps decided that Mom's throat looked like a good place to land, but after 20 hands slapped him away, he decided to move along. As he did, Stevie, with his usual enthusiasm and vigor, swung his arm back, a giant hymnal in his hand, ready to dispatch this wasp once and for all.

Now, as we were sitting there, three different scenarios flashed through our minds:

1. Stevie is actually going to hit this wasp, sending the **now-angry insect** down into the crowd below.

2. Stevie is going to miss the wasp (more likely), but will accidentally throw that **hymnal** down into the crowd below.

3. Stevie is going to miss the wasp entirely, but the momentum of his swing will send both **himself and the hymnal** down into the crowd below.

As you can see, none of these options turn out well for the crowd below.

Fortunately, Dad caught hold of Stevie before any of this could occur, much to our relief. Believe me, if the folks down below had known, they'd have been relieved, too!

Anyway, the service went on without a hitch, and afterwards, we got to speak to the pastor, who informed us that the wasps had built a huge nest in the north wall. "We were fortunate," he said, "it was bees a few years ago." No matter what he did to get rid of them, they always kept coming back. Therefore, he dubbed them the "Holy Ghost Wasps" and gave them a little job. With a grin, he announced, "I dare my congregation to sleep through one of my sermons." Hey, if it works, it works!

A Bee-sting Remedy

Speaking of bees, we were at a church fellowship one time in Georgia, and Sarah got stung by a bee, wasp, or yellow jacket--we're still not quite sure which. Being at a picnic, we couldn't find any baking soda or meat tenderizer to soothe the pain, so we started asking around. We were soon approached by a couple of old-timers--you know; "good old boys"--who were quick to offer us their own remedy, i.e., chewing tobacco. That's all well and good, we thought, but surely we wouldn't find *that* at a church picnic, would we? I mean, we're on church grounds, for goodness sake!

Apparently we *would,* because not five minutes after they went to see if any of the other old-timers had any, they were back with a whole pouch of the stuff. Someone had brought their "chaw" to church.

The only thing Mom and Sarah didn't anticipate was the fact that the tobacco had to be, um … well … moistened. So, when one of the old-timers yanked a wad out of his mouth and slapped it on Sarah's leg, they both almost went into hysterics. He did cover it up with a paper towel, though.

While Sarah was less than enthusiastic about putting the icky brown stuff on her skin, it did work. The **South**… you've gotta love it. Only down here can you take your chaw to church and receive thanks for it.

Our very own Mississippi Squirrel Revival

Have you ever heard the old Ray Stevens song, <u>The Mississippi Squirrel Revival</u>? If you haven't, just do yourself a favor and look it up on Google. That ought to catch you up to the rest of us. Now, are you ready? Good, 'cause I'm about to tell you about our very own squirrel revival.

We were in Pennsylvania one time at a camping community, where we would be performing later that week. One of the families had graciously allowed us the use of their quaint little cabin, so we were settling in for our first night there. Everyone was dispersing to their respective bedrooms when Michelle noticed a little gray "something" running into Stevie and Michael's bedroom. Because she was such a good sister, and because, well, she wanted to get some sleep that night, she went to investigate. She looked for it for a few minutes, and quickly determined that it was some kind of rodent, though it was moving too fast for her to identify.

So, she called out the Weaver "Swat Team," comprised of herself, Sam, and Jimmy. For the good of the family, they made an executive decision to exterminate the rodent. Armed with two brooms, a wooden dowel, a knife, and a shoe, they stepped into the tiny room and closed the door.

(Now, this next part of the story has been supplied by eyewitness accounts ... what we actually heard from outside the door, and a bit of my own imagination, as I wasn't actually in the room when this event occurred. Where was I, you ask? Well, I was located outside the door, interceding on the poor rodent's behalf ... and hiding, of course.)

Michelle, Sam, and Jimmy were standing in the middle of the room, when all of a sudden, this little gray blur streaks out from underneath the bed and leaps from the floor to the wall to the ceiling and back again. Obviously, we're not dealing with your everyday, ordinary rat. Maybe it's Mighty Mouse. Whatever it is, it has now been dubbed the Unidentified Flying Rodent (UFR).

Before they could even react, the UFR launches itself into the middle of the group, and it's the Mississippi Squirrel Revival all over. The UFR charges at Sam, who grabs his broom and does a remarkable imitation of a drunken witch trying to take off in a tornado. Jimmy and his broom immediately jump up on the bed to get a better look, and plan the next attack, no doubt. Michelle tries to stay out of the way of Sam's flight … I mean, fight.

The UFR, sensing that he's outnumbered and outweighed, retreats to the tiny, open closet in the corner of the room. Sam, who has sufficiently recovered, is the first one there, followed closely by Michelle. Jimmy is still on the bed, calling out support and instructions.

Now, I see this as a practical joke from God, but you'll have to make up your own mind. At this point, the window falls open, causing the curtain to float up and skitter down the entire length of Jimmy's arm. I'm still not sure how that window survived. If Jimmy had had his way, it wouldn't have. He whirled around and just about whacked that window as hard as he could, in a panic induced by visions of 6-foot rats coming to the aid of their little rodent relative, no doubt. Michelle snapped him out of it just in time to save the window. Crisis diverted. Back to the closet.

Sam is now in the closet, looking around for the little thing, when it falls at his feet. He finally gets a good look at it.

Sam: "Wait, that's not a rat. Hey, it's kind of cute. Where'd it go?"

UFR skitters to the top of a stack of linens, blankets, and pillows, stopping when he's eye-level with Sam.

Sam (a little behind): "I wonder what it … whoa, it's charging AT MY FACE!!!"

He starts swinging his broom wildly. Jimmy, (yep, still on the bed) yells, "Get him, Sam!" and runs across the bed to assist him. Sam backs out of the closet, swinging his broom, while Jimmy charges forward, swinging his broom and jumping off the bed. BOOM! They collide and go down in a pile of flailing limbs; Jimmy trying to climb over Sam to the closet, and Sam trying to get away from both Jimmy and the closet. At this point, Michelle collapses in hysterical laughter. (Well, what would you do?)

Now is as good a time as any to regroup. Now that they know that the UFR isn't an ugly rat, a rodent of unusual size, or any other potentially hazardous creature, their moods change. They decide to capture it, which, in my opinion, is much better than their first plan, which was to send it to the big nut bowl in the sky. It is a cute little **flying squirrel**, after all.

In the meantime, the group of us downstairs are getting kind of worried about the screaming, yelling, and pounding around that's going on up there. Michelle runs from the room to find some sort of capturing implement, and she explains the situation as we help her look for something. The best we can come up with is a clear plastic tote that had previously housed a selection of snacks from our hosts. She empties it and returns to the battlefield.

Back upstairs, the boys have wedged a sheet of cardboard against the opening of the closet to impede the UFR's escape route. Then, they see it. Michelle gets back just in time to see a collective twelve feet and 400 pounds of young men trying to stuff themselves into a four-foot closet ... their intent being to seek out and capture a four-inch, two ounce flying squirrel. Obviously, it isn't working, so they squeeze back out for another try.

Jimmy (finally off the bed) pokes around a little, then whispers, "Freeze!" There it is on the floor. "Oh, it's cute! Quick," he whisper-shouts, "hand me the tote!" It's passed to him. Hoisting the tote over his head, he drops it on top of the flying squirrel and stands on it.

The UFR does his impression of a pinball in a pinball machine ... ping, ping, ping, ping! A cheer goes up! Success! We caught it!

The celebration is short-lived. Now what? How are we gonna get it out of the cabin? Dad is called in for counsel. The rest of us are bumped up against the door, listening as hard as we can. (If a practical joker had swung open the door, pointed at the floor, and screamed, there would have been a stampede that would have claimed at least one small child's life.)

Jimmy stands guard (literally) as the others find something to slide under the tote. All they can find is a doormat. Not perfect, but it'll work. Minutes tick by as the doormat is slid under the tote, then the lid is slid in under the doormat. Finally the doormat is slid out. The lid snaps on and another cheer goes up as the captive is paraded downstairs. The squirrel is doing his equivalent of banging on a cell door and screaming, "I'm innocent, ya hear me? Innocent!" As he protests, he is escorted out of the cabin and into the woods. There, he was humanely released out into the wild. Steve Irwin would have been so proud.

Everyone went home happy that night--even the squirrel, though he will probably need years of therapy. Ah, another day--another swat callout.

Snake Handlers

Now, hearing about all of these adventures may have some of you wondering if we've ever dealt with any "snake handlers" in all of our travels. For all of you who are fortunate enough not to know, "snake-handling" is an act of "faith" in many backwoods, country churches. Rattlesnakes, safely milked of their venom, of course, (yeah, right) are collected during the week and placed in aluminum flour cans, usually located underneath the pulpit. (Just in case you're wondering, that's the first place to look … if you see a can and it rattles, you'd better run while you still can!)

Anyway, on Sunday, those snakes get to come out and play. Apparently, if your "faith" is strong enough, you can hold, touch, and handle those rattlers without getting bitten. Right. I can't help but wonder … um, what happens if your faith isn't strong enough? Does Matthew 4:7 or Luke 4:12 come to mind at all? You know, the "You shall not tempt the Lord your God" part?!?

Anyway, to answer your initial question: "No, we've never had the opportunity to play at one of those churches." Leastways, we've never been to one that actually brought them out.

I can tell you right now how that would turn out. They'd be on their feet, whooping and hollering and passing out the snakes, and there'd be a ten-person conga line heading out the front door. That, or they'd have ten new back doors. Their choice! It's not all that common anymore, thank goodness, or I'd be forsaking the gathering of the brethren--know what I mean?

Well, that concludes our adventures with nature up to this point. This, if nothing else, should convince you that God has a sense of humor. We sure believe it.

Surviving the Revival

CHAPTER SIXTEEN

Lasting Impressions

People tend to think a number of things when they first meet us. *Who are these people? How many are there? Why are they all dressed the same? Why are they all tackling Stevie?* (Well, maybe not that last one so much, but you get my gist.) However, it's what they think about *after* they've gotten to know us that is the focus of this chapter.

Believe me, we've heard plenty of what people think of us over the years. First impressions, random thoughts, confessions of prejudices made before meeting us … you name it, we've probably heard it. Some of it is good, some of it isn't so good. Let me share with you some of our most memorable ones:

"When I heard you were coming, I really didn't want to come, because I *hate* Southern Gospel music … (long, dramatic pause) … but I *loved* you guys!" --Woman in Georgia

"I wasn't gonna come to church today, but y'all were worth getting off the couch and getting dressed up for!"--Woman in Georgia

"We usually *hate* bluegrass music, but we love y'all!"-- Too many different people and places to count.

(By the way, the right way to answer in any situation like this is to smile and nod. Yep, that's the universally acceptable reaction for when you don't know quite what to say. So, the next time you see someone just nodding and smiling, you can be pretty sure that something interesting just happened.)

While these impressions are definitely more entertaining to hear, I also want to share a few of the more serious impressions that people have told us-- especially some of the pastors:

"You see a lot of Christian singers, and you see a lot of entertainers out there. You don't see many "Christian entertainers," but that's what you and your family are."--Man in Georgia

"What a blessing to know the Weaver family singers! They are friends of mine. If you like Gospel music with bluegrass blended in, you are in for a real treat. I call the Weavers the 'von Trapps of Southern Gospel music'. They are truly unique. Remember how your heart was warmed and affirmed when you first watched

The Sound of Music? This couple and their eight beautiful children (each one plays an instrument) will bring that same special warmth and joy to your church. Your fellowship will be all smiles with their faith-affirming, enthusiastic outlook and genuine love for the Lord." -- Dr. Charles J. Thomas, First Baptist Church, McDonough, Georgia

"I am happy to recommend the Weaver family and their ministry. I have known their faithfulness to the Lord over the past twenty years. Their arrangement of music is mostly Southern Gospel, and is performed with hearts that reflect a genuine love for Christ and His church. The unique thing about them is that, in a day when families are often pulled apart by a variety of commitments and goals, they have pulled together as a family to minister to others. You will be encouraged by their warm-hearted family presentation of Gospel music." -- Pastor Hal Wynn, Northside Baptist Church, N. Fort Myers, Florida

"I recommend this great family. The Weavers will be a blessing to your church or any Christian work. There is no family their equal in Gospel music. They have a wonderful testimony for our Lord." -- Rev. Charles W. Webb, Stone Pile Baptist Church, Clarkesville, Georgia

"I have known Paul Weaver and his family for over 20 years. They were members of my church for many years. The children are some of the finest people I have ever known. I had the privilege of baptizing several of them … they are home-schooled, and have learned to walk together and serve the Lord as a family. You will be blessed by the Weaver family." -- Doug Merck, Director of Missions, White County, Georgia Georgia Baptist Convention

"The Weaver Believer Survival Revival was a big hit…as I have visited in homes and hospitals, so many of our people have commented on what a wonderful time they had, largely due to the ministry of the Weaver family. Their music was traditional, but inspiring and uplifting. Our people adored their children. They all have wonderful personalities, and several of our ladies threatened to take the younger ones home. They are coming back in October. I highly recommend them for your special event." -- Pastor Mike Harbin, 1st Baptist Church, Lovejoy, Georgia

(We even got our pastor to write something for us):

"It is with a great sense of joy and privilege that I recommend the "Weaver Believer Survival Revival" family. Paul Weaver and his family are precious people in the Lord. As their pastor, there are many things that I could say as to why you should have them come and minister in your church or fellowship. For the sake of time, allow me to share three things that I believe set them apart:

First, they have a love for the Lord Jesus Christ. All of their family has a deep devotion for Christ and His

132

Church. Paul has shared so many times the reason they are out there singing is because God has called them to do it. They feel a true calling to obey Him and that He receive all of the glory for whatever the family accomplishes and does. They sacrifice, work, and have a passion to sing because they love Jesus. When they are not singing, they are strong supporters in the ministry of our local church.

Secondly, they love each other. There are ten of them, so they are known for the size of their family. Yet, just spending time with them, you see that it is the size of their heart that sets them apart. Their love for each other in turn gives them a great love for others. Since I have been their pastor, they have been a great source of encouragement to me. They are just a blessing to be around.

And third, God has blessed them with tremendous talent. You will be blessed by their harmony and their heart as they sing and play as a family. It is truly amazing how God has blessed this family with as many gifts as He did. God is using them to touch people in all areas of life and ministry. Let me say in closing, I know firsthand what a blessing the Weaver family is. Therefore, it is not only easy, but also a delight to recommend them to you to serve in your place of ministry." -- Pastor Michael Wilkes, Center Baptist Church, Robertstown, Georgia

Now, I'm not writing all of this down just to "toot our own horn." Honestly, I hadn't even considered it until my editor suggested a chapter about what people think and say about us and our ministry. Now that I've gotten used to the idea, I agree. I'm paraphrasing here, but Proverbs 31:31b says "Let (their) deeds publicly declare (their) praise." In other words, let their actions be their affirmation, not merely their words. Since I can't *show* you these things through the pages of a book, I'll have to settle with being a sounding board of what other people have said about us.

Of course, we go through so many different peoples' lives, even on just a weekly basis, that we can't track them all down and ask them of their impressions. However, some things have been told to us so many times that they now stand out in our memory. You'd probably be surprised at how many people come up and tell us this kind of stuff. Such as:

"Your family is so blessed."

"I can feel God's power so strongly in your ministry."

"I wish my family could have done this."

"The Lord has anointed you and your ministry."

"You guys look like you're having such a good time doing this."

"You have so much energy while you're on stage."

"I can't begin to tell you how you and your family have blessed me today."

Honestly, we hear that last one often. And seriously, when we do, we don't "blow it off." We just silently thank God, yet again, for using us. I know it sounds cliché, but it is true. And truthfully, of all the things they could be saying, we can't think of anything that we'd rather hear.

Surviving the Revival

CHAPTER SEVENTEEN

Lessons Learned

When you're in a big family like ours, you tend to learn a few memorable things along the way. And when you're involved in any kind of ministry, you tend to pick up a few lessons in that, too. So, I want to share a few of the lessons we've learned individually, and as a family. Think of it as food for thought.

1. **It's not about you**. As part of a big family, you quickly figure out that life does not revolve around you. You are a part of something bigger than yourself--your family. That also applies in the Christian life. As a child of God, you are a part of something bigger--your spiritual family. How are your thoughts, words, and actions reflecting on your family? How are they reflecting on your Father?

2. **No matter what happens, just keep singing.** Stuff happens. Distractions occur. Things that slow you down or divert your attention pop up all the time. That's as true on-stage as it is off.

It's how we let the distractions affect us that make the difference. No matter what happens, we need to keep doing what we're supposed to be doing, whether it's singing, working, or whatever. Don't let distractions knock you off-course.

3. **When God opens a door, be dumb enough to walk through it.** Yes, I know this sounds incredibly simplistic, but it holds a grain of truth. So many times, when God opens a door, we'll balk at the threshold and carefully analyze it-- wasting precious time as we over-think and try to comprehend it. When God opens a door, this should be where the "walking by faith" thing comes in. You don't have to know all the answers. You just have to take the first step.

4. **Don't wait until you have all your ducks in a row to serve the Lord.** When we started singing, we weren't perfect. We weren't even passably good. We sang to shut-ins and at nursing homes and churches--to people who couldn't escape. But you know what? Along the way, God has equipped us for exactly what we need, exactly when we need it. It doesn't happen overnight, but it does happen if you keep plodding along. Dad likes to coin this phrase: "God doesn't always call those that He's equipped, but He does equip those that He calls." In other words, if you feel God calling you to

something, don't wait until you think you're ready. Ask the Lord for His help, guidance, and blessing, then jump in head-first.

5. **It's all or nothing.** In Matthew 6:24, Jesus says that you can't serve two masters. When He said that, He meant that you can't serve both God and yourself. Someone's gotta be in the driver's seat. Who is controlling your life? You can't halfway serve the Lord. It's all or nothing.

6. **If you don't stay plugged in, you will inevitably burn out.** Do you know what happens when a hot, burning coal is separated from the fire? It cools down, getting dimmer and dimmer until it eventually goes out. It's the same in your Christian walk. If you don't stay connected through your church, prayer, and God's Word, you're going to burn out. It's not a question of "if." It's a question of "when." You and I are like rechargeable batteries; if we don't get plugged in and recharged every now and then, we're going to get exhausted and burnt out, becoming completely useless to the kingdom of God. On the other hand, the more the battery is plugged in, the better and longer the charge is. Don't let Satan fool you into thinking that you can do this on your own, especially if you are the one doing the ministering. Believe me--even ministers need to be ministered to.

7. **Don't waste your time worrying.** When there are unknowns in your future, things that you're not sure how they're going to turn out, it's incredibly easy to worry about them. God wouldn't have us worry, though. In Matthew 6:34, Jesus says, "So don't worry about tomorrow, for tomorrow will bring its own worries." Worrying about things before they happen is just wasting precious time. What can you do with that time instead of worrying?

8. **God's in control, even during the storms.** If you've been a Christian longer than fifteen minutes, you probably know this. Things won't always be hunky-dory in the Christian life. Some televangelists may promise you a happy, wonderful life if you send in a tithe to their church, but that isn't true, nor is it biblical. The Christian life is messy. It isn't easy, blissful, or perfect. Early believers were martyred, for goodness sake! As an ally of Heaven, we are going to go through hard times. That's just the way it is. And that's not all. "The rain falls on the just and the unjust," says Matthew 5:45. Bad things happen to everyone. For example: as I'm writing this book, we're going through the roughest economic recession that we've had in fifty years. Believe me, things definitely aren't easy right now. However, with all that is changing, with the world shaking around us, we still know that God is in control. We trust Him

completely to take care of us and provide for our needs. When you don't understand, just trust.

9. **Be prepared to be stretched out of your comfort zone.** Everybody has a limit to their comfort zones. Even seasoned performers, speakers, etc., have areas where they aren't comfortable, and would prefer not to be. Part of working for the Lord is allowing God to stretch you and your faith by putting you in situations that you aren't comfortable in. You'll find that these are the times that God can really work through you. When He's the only one who can do it, He does--in truly amazing ways.

10. **Expect the miraculous.** When God has a plan, He has, does, and will move mountains to accomplish it. Any story in the Bible can validate that statement. We can, too. One of the awesome perks of being a part of that plan is being able to watch it unfold. I can't begin to tell you of all the miracles that we've seen God do. It's simply amazing. When you know that God is doing something through and around you, that's when you can expect the unexpected.

11. **Never underestimate the power of prayer.** As you probably can imagine, we sell CDs at every concert we perform. One of the things we ask from the stage is that if someone buys a CD from us, and while it's playing, if God brings us to

their mind, we ask that they'd say a prayer for us. There's a reason for that, too: we stand in the face of Satan in everything that we do. Having a big family, staying together as a family, being involved in a ministry--he hates these things. He hates everything about us. I honestly believe he would destroy us if God would let him. That's why prayer is so important. James 5:16b says, "The earnest prayer of a righteous person has great power and produces wonderful results." I've seen God work through the prayers of His people time and time again. That's why it's important never to underestimate that power.

12. **There is no age limit for serving the Lord.** Consider this: we've been serving the Lord for the past 10 years. When we started, we were just little kids. We didn't really know what we were doing, but we knew that God wanted us to do it. He showed us that there's no age limit for serving the Lord. You can look through the Bible and see the same thing. There are many times that God uses children and young people to do His will, not because of their talents and strengths, but just because He can and is glorified through it. So, young people, don't let your fears and intimidations keep you from being a part of God's wonderful plan. You'll never regret letting Him have control.

13. Pastors are people, too. We spend a lot of time with pastors in our line of work. Pastors are probably the most under-appreciated leaders of our time. Sometimes it's easy for us to forget that pastors are human, too. They're just doing the best that they can, and trusting God for the rest. We church-goers need to support and encourage our pastors, rather than nag, bully, or torment them. Even if we may not agree with them, we need to keep them lifted up in prayer. They deserve at least that much.

14. It's not over 'til it's over. We sing to a lot of older folks, and we hear this excuse often: "My children are gone, my family is gone, I must be finished serving the Lord." Well, we tell this to audiences all the time: "If God was finished with you, you wouldn't be here anymore." It's that simple. If God didn't have any other use for you down here, He'd take you home. Well, if you're reading this, you're obviously still here, so … what does God have for you to do? Are you looking for His opportunities?

15. It's okay to be different. Let's face it, everybody likes to fit in. Why else would people, especially young people, proclaim, "Treat me like an individual!" and then dress, talk, and act like everybody else their age? "Fitting in" is good, but only to a point. Romans 12:2 says, "Do not conform to the pattern of this world, but be transformed by the renewing of your mind." In other words, we as Christians should be standing out of the crowd, even if it's just by our thoughts, actions, and mindsets. No, I'm not saying to go shave your head and tattoo Jesus' face on it, or to wear religious t-shirts all the time. But, we as Christians need to be willing to take a stand when it's necessary.

16. **There's nothing like serving the Lord.** It's that simple. The blessings you receive far outweigh the sacrifices you make. It's all worth it to be in the center of His will.

Well, I'm sure we've learned more than this, but it would take another book to tell you about it all. I hope that this will be a little reminder of all the things that God has taught us. Maybe He's taught you the same things. Maybe He wants you to learn some of them. What lesson is God teaching you today?

AND FINALLY ...

One more story...

Up Close and Personal

In all honesty, I debated long and hard about whether or not to include this personal note to you. But, it is my personal testimony about what God has brought me through, and I thought you should know it. Part of me is very afraid that it's going to come across wrong, and that you'll miss the point entirely. And, honestly, I don't like to expose my "vulnerable" side. Few people do. But, I'm going to do it anyway because I feel like God wants me to, so please bear with me.

I don't know quite how to say this, so I'm just going to blurt it out. **"If it had been up to me alone, I would not be with the band today. Not even remotely close to it."**

Surprised?

Well, perhaps I should start at the beginning:

People ask me all the time: "Where do you see yourself in five years?" Boy, is that a loaded question. You see, a few years ago, I had the next five years of my life planned out perfectly. I was graduating from high school that year (2007). I had picked out the colleges I wanted to attend, and I had the grades to get me there. I was going to major in Professional Writing, Creative Writing, or English, with a minor in Advertising. I planned to get a job at a publishing house or an advertising firm when I graduated, no matter what I had to do, or where I had to move to make it happen.

Let me tell you right now, singing wasn't in the arrangement. I mean, sure, it was okay for a hobby while I was at home, but it wasn't my passion. Now that I was finally getting my wings, I could pursue my own dreams -- my own life. If the band wanted to continue without me, that was fine with me. Good luck to them, but "I'm out of here!"

Then, in the midst of all that planning and preparation, I had an encounter with God. I didn't want to. I tried not to. But He got through anyway. He told me that I had a decision to make. I'd been making the plans for my life, He pointed out; all I wanted from Him was the blessing. *"Here are my plans, Lord, just bless them and we'll be fine."* He showed me in several consecutive ways that His plans for my life didn't include college at that time. His plans for me included

146

staying with the band ... indefinitely. If I wanted to be in the center of His will, I would have to surrender my dreams and plans. If I wanted to go my own way, then I'd have to do it without His blessing.

If I told you that I surrendered right then and there like a good little Christian, saying "Yes, Lord, Thy will be done," in my most humble, spiritual voice, I'd be lying. On the contrary. God and I wrestled back and forth over this issue for almost a month. These were my hopes and dreams we were talking about -- things I'd been preparing for since Junior High. These were things that young adults all over the world were dreaming of... why couldn't I? How could God ask me to give them up? Didn't He understand the sacrifice involved? How could I just walk away from my future plans?

It took a long, long time, but I finally got to the point where I knew that I didn't want to do anything without being in the center of God's will. No, it wasn't an easy decision to make. I reached that point through endless weeks of tears, sleepless nights, and serious soul-searching. It was the hardest decision I've ever made in my life.

So I stayed. When my friends and peers went on without me, it felt like a dagger in my heart, but I stayed. I couldn't tell you all the times I cried myself to sleep, mourning the death of my future. But I stayed.

147

Anger and bitterness fought for the possession of my soul. But I stayed.

For a while, I didn't know what I was supposed to do. After working so hard for so long towards my plans, I was at a loss. Now what? I did the only thing I knew to do -- keep singing. I'm not going to lie. The days, weeks, and months following the decision were some of the hardest of my life. I'd do okay for a while, then someone would ask me how my college plans were coming, and everything would come rushing back. Since the option of not going to college wasn't smiled upon by many people, I also had to deal with the judgments of others. Their well-meant lectures on the importance of education were meant to be helpful and inspiring, I'm sure. But to me, they were just salt in the wound.

As you might expect, this is the hardest story I've had to tell in this entire book. Dredging up all of these memories is much harder than I thought it would be. But it *does* get better. You see, God had to bring me to a breaking point, a point of total surrender, before He could really start working in me.

No matter what happened, though, God was with me. I felt His presence more in that time than I ever had before. We took it a day, sometimes an hour, sometimes a moment, at a time. I fervently prayed for a calling to sing and share His message through music. If this is what He wanted, I needed a passion for it, or my soul was going to wither away. It didn't come immediately. It didn't come in one day or one week. Slowly but surely, it came when I least expected it.

Well, now you've heard how much I thought I had lost during that whole turbulent time. Today, as I read through the entries I made in my journal following that time, I can't help but look back and marvel at how much I was gaining from the whole experience.

In the next months and, eventually years, my relationship with God grew more than it ever had before. It was a hard, bumpy road. Looking back now, though, that alone would have been worth every bit of it. When I learned to depend on Him for everything, He proved Himself, and provided what I needed, again and again. He gave me the strength, peace, and joy to make it through the tough times. He gave me grace and patience to wait, even though it was hard. He gave me stronger, better relationships with my family. More than that, He gave me a heart for what I do. Rarely does a concert go by where I don't get choked up as I sing of God's grace and providence. I can't help it. He overwhelms me.

I'm not sure how this testimony fits with the rest of the book, but maybe somebody somewhere needs to hear it. Sometimes, all God wants is an unconditional surrender. When you submit entirely to His will, that's when He can use you beyond anything you could even imagine. When I look back on it now, all I can tell you is this. If this is the only thing you remember from all that I have written, I hope it's this:

It was worth it.

In the end, it was all worth it. All the heartache, pain, and sacrifices were worth it. It's all worth it to be in the center of His will. There's nothing like it in the world. I know it's hard to comprehend, but I've never felt so free in my life. I know beyond a shadow of a doubt that God has everything under control and that His plans are better than anything I could ever imagine.

Am I saying that I no longer have bad days and wonder when my dreams will ever come to pass? No, absolutely not. But, Matthew 6:33 (KJV) says "Seek ye <u>first</u> the kingdom of God and His righteousness, <u>then</u> all these things will be added unto you." When you put Him first, you can hold Him to His promise that He'll take care of everything else.

And guess what? It has all come full-circle. The main college I was applying to dropped many of its majors, including the Professional Writing, and closed its campus doors to undergraduate students last year. That means I would have been forced to leave during my sophomore year, before I even got close to taking the writing classes. (And if you still don't think God knows what He's doing, keep reading.)

A few months ago, we were at a church in Florida on a Sunday night, singing just another show, when the pastor of the church came up and started talking to Mom afterwards. As they talked, she learned that he was one of the co-founders of an on-line community college. When he asked if anyone was taking college courses, she gave him the usual answer: "No, not at this point in time." What happened next can only be described as a miracle.

As they talked, it came out that I had wanted to take classes for over a year and a half, but hadn't had the opportunity with all the traveling and finances involved. When he heard this, he immediately called me over and made me an offer. He said he would get me into the Associate's degree program at his college for the cost of textbooks and registration -- nothing more. Tuition would be free. After I finished there, he'd make sure that my transcripts could be transferred to wherever I wanted to finish out my Bachelor's degree. At this point, it looks like Liberty University.

I asked for some time to finish writing this book, and he graciously gave it to me. As soon as I'm done with it, I'm scheduled to start taking on-line courses at his college.

Not only that, but I've actually *written* a book! Me! With no real instruction or experience to speak of, with no credentials or anything. God has given me the desires of my heart, through His own timing and to His own glory.

And you know what? He'll do the same for you. All that's required is obedience. I know I've said it before, but it is so true. Even if these plans all fall to pieces tomorrow, I'll still be able to cling to the fact that He has everything under control and will provide another way.

So now, when people ask me where I see myself in five years, I can honestly say I have no idea. I don't even know where I'm going to be in the next five weeks. I'm okay with that, though. I've learned not to plan too far in the future. I'll trust God for whatever happens, regardless of the outcome.

So, it all comes down to a question of surrender. I've written several pages in an attempt to express to you this vital spiritual concept. J. W. Van Defender penned a hymn that said it in 3 sentences:

> *I surrender all.*
> *I surrender all.*
> *All to thee, my blessed savior,*
> *I surrender all.*

I don't know what tomorrow brings, but I know in which direction I'm headed, and I know who holds my hand. Everything changed the day I surrendered my life to Him.

The question is, will you? My prayer is that you will!

Surviving the Revival

And so it ends ...

Well, we've made it to the end of our journey. There were times when I wasn't sure that we would, but we did. It's time to say goodbye.

Before you close this book, though, I just wanted to thank you for tagging along on this adventure with me. I hope it was entertaining, but more than that, I hope it was thought-provoking. I sincerely pray that God will speak to you or maybe challenge you through this insignificant collection of stories. If He does, it'll be entirely through Him, not through anything I could do. That's merely one of the things that is so amazing about Him.

May God bless you as you travel on the path He has laid out for you. If He gave you the strength to start it, He'll give you the strength to finish it--just ask Him.

Until we meet again,

Anna

Surviving the Revival

About the Author

Anna discovered her love for writing at a very early age, when she wrote and entered a story in the local library's short story contest. When it won "first place," her discovery was affirmed. In high school, one of her short stories received an "Honorable Mention" in Bob Jones University's "Inscriptions" annual writing competition.

Anna has been performing with her family since the age of 14. Prior to that, she sang in church musicals, kids' choir, and for special occasions, before she went full-time with her family at age 16. Now at age 21, she sings and plays the acoustic bass guitar in the band. The flexibility of on-line college classes gives her the opportunity to further her education while still traveling in full-time ministry.

She lives in the mountains of North Georgia with her family and pets.

Surviving the Revival

If you want to contact Anna, you can reach her at surviving<u>therevival@yahoo.com</u>.

If you want to learn more about the Weaver Believer Survival Revival, please visit <u>www.WeaverBeliever.com</u>.

Surviving the Revival

3519443

Made in the USA